CANINE COUTURE

CANINE COUTURE

25 projects: fashion and lifestyle accessories for designer dogs

Lilly Shahravesh

Photography by VANESSA DAVIES

jacqui small

First published in 2008 by Jacqui Small LLP
7 Greenland Street
London NW1 0ND

Publisher Jacqui Small
Commissioning Editor Zia Mattocks
Art Director Sarah Rock
Production Peter Colley

ISBN: 978 1 906417 09 3

2010 2009 2008
10 9 8 7 6 5 4 3 2 1
Printed in Singapore

CONTENTS

INTRODUCTION

Five years ago my sister came home with Missy, the sweetest toy dog I'd ever seen. Missy is half Chihuahua and half miniature pinscher, and, although tiny, she has the biggest personality: she isn't just a dog; she is a member of the family. However hard I looked for gifts to pamper her with, I could never find anything that was good enough for her. We all like quality, style and design, so why can't we find that for our pets? Why should our four-legged loved ones be treated as second-rate? After the frustration of not being able to find anything good enough for Missy, I started making her gifts myself, which was the beginning of Lovemydog.

When I set up my business, pet gifts were almost unheard of. It was tough getting shop buyers to take me seriously and recognize that there was a market for high-quality pet products because there really were people like me who wanted stylish accessories for their pets. My belief in what I do – and the chance to combine my love of dogs and fabrics – is what has motivated me to keep pushing on with the business. My inspiration comes from all around – from the things I see in the street every day; from the dogs I meet and the places I visit. I love colour, textures, traditional fabrics (which I hoard endlessly), fashion, art, photography and the beautiful British countryside. I choose natural fabrics for my designs whenever I can, and I love the qualities of pure wool and the feel of natural cotton fabrics. I'm lucky enough to love what I do, and there isn't anything in the Lovemydog collection that I wouldn't use myself. My terrier Rabbit and his doggy friends are always game for trying out the products I design.

You don't need to buy expensive fabrics. Old offcuts or scraps that you have around, old blankets, curtains, duvet covers, tea towels, clothing – basically anything you have lying around can be turned into something beautiful for your dog. One of my favourite techniques is appliqué, which is great for using up small scraps. The real beauty of appliqué is that it can make items really personal and give a splash of colour to the plainest fabric at an affordable price.

I have tried to keep the projects in this book as simple as possible, to suit all levels of sewing skills. Some are easier than others, though, so I suggest you read the instructions through before you embark on a project. Remember that there are no hard-and-fast rules, and you can make the products your own way – the steps are there as an outline, to give you the basis for something that you can truly personalize for you and your dog. You don't need a state-of-the-art sewing machine – everything in this book was made on my basic old sewing machine or sewn by hand.

The projects cover most occasions, so there's something for every dog – whether it's for indoors, outdoors or just for fun, you'll find projects that will inspire and motivate you. There may be something particular to you and your dog's routine that you want to create, in which case you can adapt any of the projects in the book to suit, and express your dog's personality through the design, the decoration and the colours you choose.

Enjoy working with the fabrics, and don't worry if the finish isn't perfect – handmade items have a charm of their own, and that's what makes them special. What matters the most is the enjoyment of making something yourself that is really special for you and your dog.

LILLY (www.lovemydog.biz)

EVERYDAY ESSENTIALS

The following projects will all make the day-to-day jobs a pleasure and more fun. You can create your own personalized food mat, so you don't have to put up with an uninspiring shop-bought one. Or make your own toy bag, which keeps your house nice and tidy, and looks great, too. You can even look chic on a walk with the smart pooper-scooper bag. Bring some style and splashes of colour to those everyday chores.

PERSONALIZED FOOD MAT

No matter how big a bowl I use to feed my dog, he seems to love to take the food out of it, put it on the floor and chew it there. This laminated food mat helps to protect the floor and is easy to wipe clean after he's finished, so he can make as much mess on it as he likes. This is a lovely project to make as a gift for a dog-loving friend, too, so have fun with the design and enjoy making it. I chose a mix of fabric scraps and paper for the decoration, but you can stick to just one or the other if you prefer – it's really flexible, and you can make it as individual as you want. Add your dog's photograph or his name or initials, as well as pictures of some of his favourite things.

MATERIALS

- Magazine cuttings
- Scissors for fabric and paper, or a craft knife
- Tracing paper and sharp pencil
- Thin card for templates
- Fabric scraps for appliqué shapes
- Photograph of your dog
- Plain fabric for the food mat backing, 41 x 29cm
- Decorative bias binding, 2cm wide
- Pins
- Sewing machine
- Contrasting sewing thread for the topstitch
- Glue for paper and fabric
- Needle

PREPARING THE DECORATIVE MOTIFS

Cut out any pictures from magazines that you like. If there is a particular image that you may want to reuse, make a good-quality colour photocopy of it first, so that you can reuse it as often as you wish. Choose the motifs and/or initials you would like to use to decorate your food mat (see page 138) and resize them on a photocopier. Using tracing paper and a sharp pencil, trace your chosen motifs and/or initials. Make card templates of these, then use the templates to cut the shapes from your fabric scraps (**see picture 1**). Finally, find a flattering photograph of your dog.

MAKING UP THE FOOD MAT BACKING

Cut out the main piece of fabric for the food mat backing, measuring 41 x 29cm. Pin the bias binding all around the edges of the fabric rectangle to make a decorative border. Cut the bias binding at each corner, and fold the raw edge under diagonally to make a neat join in the corners. Once the tape is pinned into place, topstitch with contrasting thread all the way around on the sewing machine, stitching two lines 2–3mm from the inner and outer edge of the bias binding (**see picture 2**).

ARRANGING THE DECORATIVE MOTIFS

Place your chosen shapes on the backing fabric. Mix up the fabric motifs with the paper shapes, and play around with the placement of all the decorative elements until you feel happy with the overall effect. Glue the shapes into position, using fabric or paper glue as applicable.

ADDING EMBROIDERY DETAIL

To lift the design further, incorporate decorative stitching. Select two or three fabric shapes on your food mat, and hand-sew around the edges with the topstitch thread. Work simple straight stitch, as I have, or blanket stitch, if you wish (**see picture 3**). Work a few of the same stitch lines on the background fabric, too, to tie in the design.

FINISHING YOUR FOOD MAT

When you have finished decorating your food mat, have it colour-photocopied at a good printer, then laminate the colour copy to protect it and ensure that it is easy to wipe clean (**see picture 4**).

> TIP: Keep your original design and, after a period of time, you can get it colour-photocopied and laminated again, or alter the decorative elements to update the design when you feel like a change, keeping the food mat backing the same.

TIDY-TOYS BAG

Decorated with appliquéd motifs, the Tidy-Toys Bag looks great and will help to keep your dog's toys in one place and your home tidy. It's a fun bag that can be very stimulating for your dog at playtime. I have taught my dog to fetch toys of his choice from his bag and bring them out to play with. He loves pushing his nose inside and choosing what attracts him at any particular moment. The bag is soft and flexible for moving around from room to room, so you can leave it wherever your dog is at the time. It also packs away neatly in a suitcase for travelling – it's very comforting for dogs to have some of their familiar toys when they are in new surroundings, whether on holiday or staying with friends.

MATERIALS
- Fabric of your choice for the bag panel, 88 x 52cm
- Tape measure
- Scissors for paper and fabric
- Sewing machine and thread
- Tracing paper
- Thin card for templates
- Sharp pencil or fabric-marker pen
- Fabric scraps for appliqué decoration
- Iron-on adhesive
- Iron, ironing board and ironing cloth
- Pins
- Backing paper for the appliqué
- Large safety pin
- 1.5m cotton cord/string

CUTTING OUT THE FABRIC

Cut out a rectangle measuring 88 x 52cm from the main bag fabric. If you would prefer to make a smaller bag, adjust the size accordingly. Overlock or zigzag-stitch around all the cut edges to help make the finished bag harder-wearing and prevent the fabric from fraying.

CREATING THE APPLIQUÉ MOTIFS

Choose the decorative motifs for your toy bag (see page 138), and make card templates of these. I used two dog shapes, two circles and a heart near the top of the bag, and an initial, two hearts and a circle near the opposite bottom corner. Iron adhesive backing

onto the wrong side of your appliqué fabric, and trace around the outline of the templates with a sharp pencil or fabric-marker pen (*see picture 1*). Cut out the appliqué motifs using sharp fabric scissors, cutting just on the inside of your drawn outline.

ARRANGING THE APPLIQUÉ MOTIFS

Fold the bag fabric in half widthways with wrong sides together, and place the fold on the left and the cut edges on the right. Mark the area you wish to decorate with appliqué embroidery, leaving the seam allowance required for the bottom and side seams (1.5–2cm) and for the drawstring casing at the top (1cm for the hem and 6–7cm for the casing) clear. Arrange the motifs on the front of the bag. When you are happy with their positions, peel off the paper backing and pin them in place (*see picture 2*). Iron the motifs to fuse the fabrics together, using a cloth to protect the fabrics from the hot iron.

SEWING THE APPLIQUÉ MOTIFS IN PLACE

Place a piece of paper behind the fabric to give it extra support. Set your sewing machine to a close satin stitch, and machine-stitch neatly around the edges of all of the appliqué motifs. Peel away the paper backing (*see picture 3*), then trim the ends of the thread to neaten the right side of the work (*see picture 4*).

MAKING UP THE BAG

Open up the main bag fabric and, with the wrong side facing you, fold down, pin and machine-stitch a 1cm hem along the top of the panel.

Fold the bag panel in half widthways with right sides together, and place a couple of marker pins 6–7cm down from the top of the bag on the open side seam. Using a 1.5–2cm seam allowance, pin and then machine-stitch the side seam, sewing from the bottom of the bag up to the marker pins (*see picture 5*).

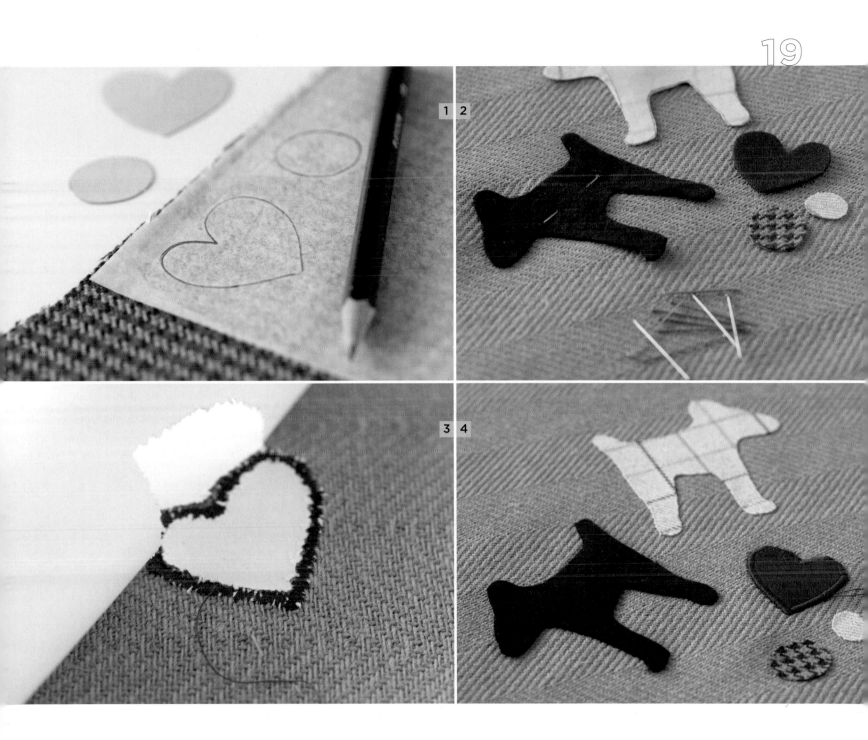

5 6

7 8

Press the side seam open, and iron down each 6–7cm section of the hem allowances at the top of the bag above the sewn side seam. Pin in place, then machine-stitch down each hem, sewing approximately 3mm from the folded edge (*see picture 6*).

Using a 1.5–2cm hem allowance, pin and then machine-stitch along the bottom edge of the bag.

CREATING THE DRAWSTRING CHANNEL

Starting at the side seam, fold down the top edge of the bag, with wrong sides together, to meet the point where your side seam stitching starts. Continue folding the top edge to this point all the way around the bag. Press and pin in place, then machine-stitch all the way along the bottom edge of this hem, using an edge foot on the sewing machine (*see picture 7*).

THREADING THE DRAWSTRING THROUGH

Cut the required length of cotton cord or string – you will need twice the width of the bag, with an extra 18–20cm at each end of the cord once it measures clear of the bag. Attach a large safety pin to one end of the string and push it all the way through the casing and out through the other hole (*see picture 8*), then knot the ends.

> TIPS: I often put new fun toys and lots of healthy chews in my dog's toy bag when he is not looking, so it is always full of exciting surprises when he delves in. This keeps his level of interest up.
> • Training a new puppy to use his toy bag can help to housebreak him, as he will concentrate on his toys instead of chewing your furniture.
> • You don't need to have lots of expensive toys to entertain your dog – an old tea towel with a knot tied in it will do.

POO-BAG HOLDER

All responsible dog owners agree that it is really important to clean up after your dog. Dogs are often blamed for waste found on pavements and in public places, but it is the owner's responsibility and not the dog's. This is a fun way to encourage everyone to clean up after their pet and make the parks and pavements cleaner. The cute 'poo poo' bag is to hold your clean biodegradable poop bags and a standard pooper-scooper, if you use one. I designed it because I was fed up with having plastic bags in my handbag, coat pockets and just about everywhere else. It is small enough to fit in your handbag, and I usually hang mine up next to my dog's lead so that I never leave home without it.

MATERIALS

- Fabric of your choice for the bag, 45 x 26cm
- Tape measure
- Scissors for paper and fabric
- Sewing machine and thread
- Tracing paper
- Thin card for templates
- Sharp pencil or fabric-marker pen
- Fabric scraps for the appliqué decoration
- Iron-on adhesive
- Iron, ironing board and ironing cloth
- Pins
- Backing paper for the appliqué
- Safety pin
- 1m cotton cord
- Biodegradable pooper-scooper bags

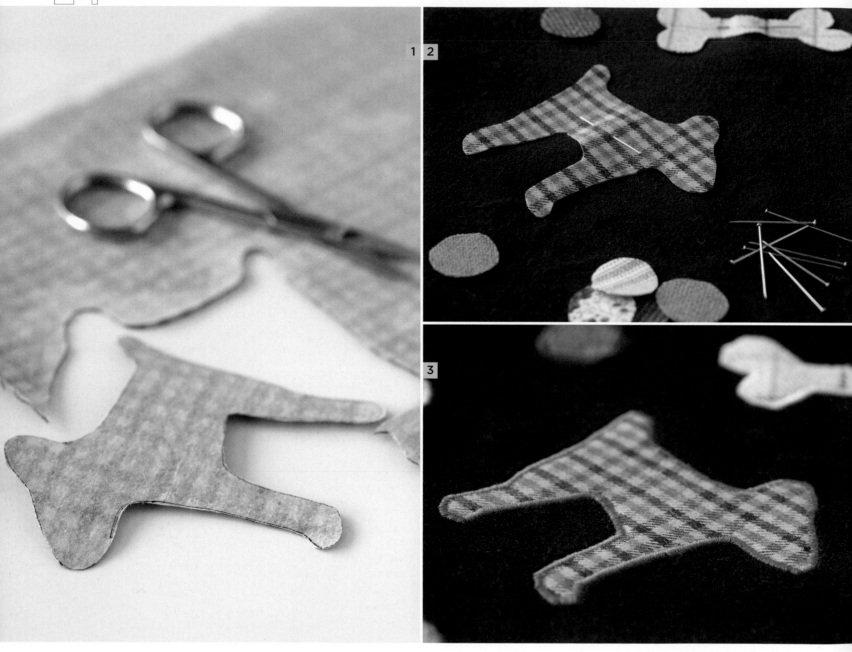

1

2

3

CUTTING OUT THE FABRIC

Cut the fabric for the bag into a rectangle measuring 45 x 26cm, and overlock or zigzag-stitch the cut edges.

CREATING THE APPLIQUÉ MOTIFS

Choose the decorative motifs for your bag (see page 138), and make card templates of these. I used a dog, bone and seven circles. Iron adhesive backing onto the wrong side of the appliqué fabrics, and trace around the templates with a sharp pencil or fabric-marker pen (**see picture 1**). Cut out the motifs using sharp fabric scissors.

ARRANGING THE APPLIQUÉ MOTIFS

Fold the bag fabric in half with wrong sides facing and short sides together, and place the fold on the left. Mark the area you wish to decorate with appliqué embroidery, remembering the seam allowance required for the bottom and side seams (1.5–2cm) and for the drawstring casing at the top (1cm for the hem and 4cm for the casing). Arrange the motifs on the front of the bag, with the dog in the centre, the bone above and the circles around them. When you are happy with the position of the shapes, peel off the paper backing and pin them in place (**see picture 2**).

SEWING THE APPLIQUÉ MOTIFS IN PLACE

Iron the motifs to fuse the fabrics together, using a cloth between the iron and the fabrics to protect them. Place a piece of paper behind the fabric to give it extra support. Set your sewing machine to a close satin stitch, and machine-stitch neatly around the edges of the motifs. Peel away the paper backing, and trim the ends of the thread to neaten the right side of the work (**see picture 3**).

MAKING UP THE POO-BAG HOLDER

The bag is made up in the same way as the Tidy-Toys Bag (see pages 18–21), with a casing allowance of 4cm plus 1cm for the hem.

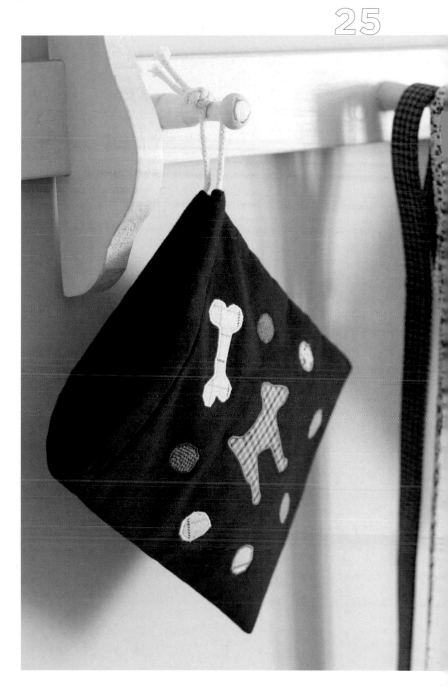

POO-BAG HOLDER

SQUEAKY TOY BONE

Toys are great for stimulating your dog and can help to build a bond between you. I love playing with my terrier Rabbit in the evenings, especially on gloomy winter days when we can't go for long walks. Unlike his friend Eddie, the Chihuahua, Rabbit is a serial shredder and is always determined to get the squeaker from inside a toy, which he does with utmost enthusiasm and concentration. He still gets enjoyment from the remains, and has endless toys that he has shredded but still adores and won't part with. These toy bones are favourites and are simple and fun to make. They are ideal for home play, too, as they won't make a noise when thrown around indoors like a heavy rubber toy would.

MATERIALS

- Pattern paper
- Sharp pencil
- Scissors for paper and fabric
- Fabric-marker pen
- Wool fabric for the front of the bone
- Sheepskin fabric for the back of the bone
- Tracing paper
- Thin card for the templates
- Iron-on adhesive
- Iron, ironing board and ironing cloth
- Fabric scraps for the appliqué decoration
- Tape measure
- Pins
- Backing paper for the appliqué
- Sewing machine and thread
- Toy stuffing
- Wooden spoon for packing the stuffing into the toy
- Toy squeakers
- Needle and thread

TEMPLATE

A12. Increase the bone template to the size you want.

CUTTING OUT THE FABRICS

First decide on your toy shape and size. You can use the bone template on page 139, increasing it to the size you want, or make your own design. Cut out a paper pattern, and place it on your chosen fabric – I used wool fabric for the top piece of the bone and sheepskin fleece for the bottom piece. Draw around the shapes with a fabric-marker pen, and cut out the top and bottom pieces. Note that the bone shapes are not symmetrical, so make sure that you cut the bottom panel out correctly so that when the wrong sides of the fabrics face each other, the shapes match.

CREATING THE APPLIQUÉ MOTIFS

Choose the decorative motifs (see page 138) and make card templates of these. Following the method described for the Tidy-Toys Bag on page 18, back your appliqué fabrics with iron-on adhesive, and cut out the motifs.

ATTACHING THE APPLIQUÉ MOTIFS

Arrange the motifs on the right side of the wool fabric, making sure there are 2–3cm clear between them and the edge of the fabric (*see picture 1*). Referring again to the instructions on page 18, peel off the backing and iron the motifs onto the fabric, then machine-stitch around the edges of the motifs using satin stitch.

JOINING THE TOP AND BOTTOM BONE SHAPES

Place the top and bottom pieces of fabric together with right sides facing, and pin, leaving a gap of 3–4cm in the centre of one side for turning the fabric through and inserting the stuffing. Mark both sides of the gap with two pins. Sew around the edge of the bone shape using small stitches on the sewing machine, so that it is tightly and securely sewn. Keep as close to the edge as possible, with a hem of 0.5–1cm, so that you retain the full bone shape. Stop at the marked points, and backstitch to reinforce the stitching (*see picture 2*).

INSERTING THE STUFFING AND SQUEAKER

Turn the shape right sides out, pushing the seams out well. Insert the stuffing, using the end of a wooden spoon, if necessary, to reach the far corners. Put a squeaker in the middle of the toy or one at each end of the bone curves. Make sure the squeaker is surrounded by stuffing, so that you can't feel any hard ridges (*see picture 3*).

CLOSING THE GAP IN THE SIDE SEAM

Once you are happy with the plumpness of the toy, fold in the hem allowance at the side opening, and carefully sew up the gap by hand with small stitches, using a needle and two strands of matching thread (*see picture 4*).

NOTE: Your dog's play with squeaker toys should be supervised at all times. If your dog removes the squeaker from the toy, take it away from him at once.

TRAINING-TREATS BAG

It is never too late to teach your dog new tricks, and it is fun to practise retrieves and other commands when out on walks. Giving rewards for good behaviour keeps your dog's attention focused on you and makes him easier to control when playing off the lead, so he's less likely to wander out of sight. You have to be the most exciting thing in his life, so that he always returns to you. This treat bag is worn across your shoulder, so you can work with hand commands and hold a treat at the same time – it also avoids your pockets getting filled with crumbs. I keep the bag full of treats at all times, and hang it on the coat hook to remind me to take it with me when I take Rabbit for a walk.

MATERIALS
- 50cm brown tweed fabric for the outer bag (minimum 148cm wide)
- 50cm yellow tweed fabric for the lining (minimum 148cm wide)
- Tape measure
- Scissors for fabric
- Hook-and-loop Velcro, 20mm wide
- Pins
- Sewing machine and thread
- Tracing paper
- Sharp pencil or fabric-marker pen
- Thin card for the templates
- Fabric scraps for the appliqué shapes
- Iron-on adhesive
- Iron, ironing board and ironing cloth
- Backing paper for the appliqué

TRAINING-TREATS BAG

CUTTING OUT THE FABRICS

Cut out two rectangles measuring 30 x 17cm, one in brown tweed for the outer bag and one in yellow tweed for the lining. Cut out one strip measuring 148 x 8cm in brown tweed for the bag strap.

SEWING ON THE VELCRO AND APPLIQUÉ MOTIFS

Pin and machine-stitch the strip of hook Velcro across one short edge of the lining and the loop Velcro across one short edge of the outer piece, approximately 2cm down.

Choose and resize the appliqué decorations (see page 138), making sure the design is no more than 6cm high or it will be covered by the bag flap, and make card templates. Following the method described for the Tidy-Toys Bag on page 18, back the appliqué fabrics with iron-on adhesive, and cut out the motifs. Arrange them on the right side of the brown tweed, at least 2cm below the Velcro. Peel off the backing, and iron the motifs to the fabric to fuse them, then machine-stitch around the edges of the motifs using satin stitch (**see picture 1**).

MAKING THE BAG STRAP

Fold the strip of brown tweed in half lengthways, and steam-press. Open the strip out again, and fold the two raw edges into the middle, lining them up with the pressed central crease, then steam-press again. Fold the strip in half again, so that the folded edges marry up and you have a long, narrow strap. Topstitch the folded edges together on the sewing machine, 2–3mm in. To create neat ends, trim the corners on the side that has been stitched, fold the raw ends of the strap into itself and hand-sew the edges neatly together (**see picture 2**).

JOINING THE BAG PANELS AND ATTACHING THE STRAP

Place the brown outer piece and the yellow lining piece with right sides together and the Velcro strips at opposite ends. Pin them together, with two pins marking a 6cm gap in the top left-hand side seam for bagging out. Using a 1cm seam allowance, stitch all the way around the rectangle, leaving a gap between the marker pins. Turn the fabric right side out through the gap, steam-press and pin the gap closed. Pin the bag strap into place on the brown outer fabric, positioning each end of the strap 2cm in from each side and 10cm down from the top edge. Stitch along the bottom of each strap and at least 3cm up each side to secure it to the main panel (**see picture 3**).

MAKING UP THE BAG

Topstitch around the bag panel, 2–3mm in from the edge, closing up the gap in the side seam.

Fold the bag panel to form a pocket, bringing the appliqué front panel up approximately 8cm from the top edge. Fold the top flap down to make sure the front panel is the right height for the Velcro to fasten, and pin it in place. Stitch down both sides of the front panel to form the pocket, sewing along the previous topstitch line for a neat finish (**see picture 4**).

TRAINING TIPS: Don't let your dog forget you are there when you are out on walks or when he is playing. Make your presence known by gently placing a treat in front of his mouth. You'll find all the other dogs will sit to attention, too, so have a few treats ready.
• If your dog ignores you after a couple of attempts at recall, turn your back on him and start running in the opposite direction, calling, 'Bye bye'. He will soon panic and come running after you. Give him a treat when he catches up with you. With practice, this gets your dog's attention and keeps his focus on you.
• Always reward your dog when he comes to you, even if it has taken you hours to get him back – never scold him. You don't have to use a treat every time; you can alternate with praise and a scratch around the ear.

COLLAR & LEAD

A stylish collar and lead are definite everyday essentials for any dog, and it's nice to have a choice of designs for use on different occasions – or even just on different days of the week or to coordinate with your outfit. In terms of fabric, you can experiment with everything from hardwearing tweed wool to crisp cotton gingham, from smart stripes to pretty floral fabric, but remember that a tightly woven cloth will be more durable. Make the collar and lead an appropriate width for the size of your dog – a small dog such as Marty the terrier can wear a 2cm-wide collar and lead, whereas a larger dog such as Holly the Labrador (see page 37) requires a more robust set 2.5cm wide.

MATERIALS

For the collar:
- Cotton string
- Fabric-marker pen
- Tape measure
- Scissors for fabric
- 50cm tightly woven wool fabric (150cm wide)
- Iron and ironing board
- 50cm webbing
- Matches
- Pins

- Sewing machine and thread
- Caveson buckle, loop and D-ring
- Fabric hole punch
- Eyelets

For the lead:
- 50cm tightly woven wool fabric (150cm wide)
- Tape measure
- Scissors for fabric

- Iron-on Interfacing
- Iron and ironing board
- 1.5m webbing
- Matches
- Sewing machine (with optional edge foot) and thread
- Square-end trigger hook

SIZING THE COLLAR

Measure your dog's neck using a piece of cotton string, and mark it in five places with a marker pen (**see picture 1**). First, mark the actual size of the neck, holding the string comfortably but snugly, then mark 2.5cm on either side of this, depending on how many eyelets you want to punch in. I recommend that the end of the collar extends by at least 10cm beyond the marker for the loosest hole. Secondly, mark where you want the loop to be placed to keep the collar excess tidy – mark this 4–6.5cm away from the last eyelet marker. Thirdly, mark another point 4–6.5cm away from the loop marker for the D-ring placement. Finally, cut the piece of string 2.5cm after the mark for the D-ring.

CUTTING OUT THE COLLAR FABRIC AND WEBBING

Cut the tweed fabric to the same length as the cotton string and the correct width to fit the buckle size, plus an extra 1.5cm hem allowance for both side edges. Fold and press down the hem on each side of the strip, ready to attach the webbing.

Cut the webbing to the same length as the tweed fabric, plus an extra 2.5cm for the tip of the collar. Using a lit match, carefully heat-seal the ends of the webbing to prevent the fabric from fraying.

BACKING THE COLLAR FABRIC WITH WEBBING

Pin the webbing onto the back of the collar fabric, overlapping it 2.5cm beyond the end. Fold the collar fabric into a point at this end and pin. Machine-stitch in place, sewing 2–3mm in from the edge along both sides of the collar and around the V shape of the pointed tip. Cut off the excess webbing around the point, and heat-seal carefully with a match (**see picture 2**).

ATTACHING THE D-RING, LOOP AND BUCKLE

Insert the straight raw end of the collar strip through the D-ring, then through the loop and finally through the buckle, using the marked piece of string to help you position each component in the correct place. Fold the fabric that extends beyond the buckle back on itself,

securing it underneath just beyond the D-ring, to keep all of the collar fittings in place. Fold in the raw edge, and pin in place (**see picture 3**).

Machine-stitch vertical lines across the collar to hold each component securely in place. Sew one vertical stitch line after the buckle, one on each side of the loop and one on each side of the D-ring. Turn the machine needle by hand if it feels too bulky under the presser foot. I recommend you sew the lines twice to make sure that it holds securely (**see picture 4**).

ATTACHING THE EYELETS

Using the marked cotton string to guide you, mark the positions for the eyelets on the collar, then punch the holes for the various neck sizes (**see picture 5**). Finally, attach eyelets (**see picture 6**).

COLLAR & LEAD

CUTTING OUT THE LEAD FABRIC AND INTERFACING

Cut out two strips in your chosen fabric to twice the required width and to a minimum length of 130cm. For a finished lead width of 3cm, cut out two strips 6cm wide. Cut four pieces of iron-on interfacing to the same width, two approximately 20cm long (for the handle end of the lead) and two approximately 5cm long (for the trigger-hook end of the lead).

BACKING THE FABRIC WITH IRON-ON INTERFACING

Iron a large piece of interfacing onto one end of a tweed strip, on the wrong side of the fabric, and iron a small piece of interfacing onto the other end of the same strip.

Do the same on the other strip of tweed. Fold the edges of each strip into the centre, with wrong sides together, so that the edges meet in the middle, and steam-press firmly (*see picture 1*).

ATTACHING THE WEBBING AND MAKING UP THE LEAD

Cut one piece of webbing to the width of the folded fabric (in this case, 3cm) and to the length of the central section of the strip, not including the sections backed with interfacing (in this case, the webbing is approximately 105cm long). Carefully heat-seal the cut ends of the webbing using a match.

Sandwich the webbing between both layers of fabric, with the right sides facing outwards, and pin in place (*see picture 2*). Machine-stitch all the way down both edges to seal the webbing inside the outer fabric, sewing 2–3mm in from each side edge – this will be easier if you use an edge foot on the sewing machine.

FORMING THE HANDLE

Tuck in the raw edge of the fabric at the handle end, with a hem allowance of at least 2.5cm. Next, fold over approximately 10cm of the lead to form the handle, and pin in place – you will know how much to fold over for the handle, as you will feel where the webbing stops inside the lead (*see picture 3*). Stitch the join securely on the sewing machine to hold it in place, sewing it twice across, then 2.5cm up each side edge and across again to make it really secure (*see picture 4*). If the lead feels bulky under the sewing-machine foot, turn the needle by hand to sew it down.

SECURING THE TRIGGER HOOK

Wrap the other end of the lead fabric around the trigger hook, and tuck in the raw edge by at least 2.5cm before folding the end under, as above. Machine-stitch in place, sewing it twice to make it really secure, as for the handle.

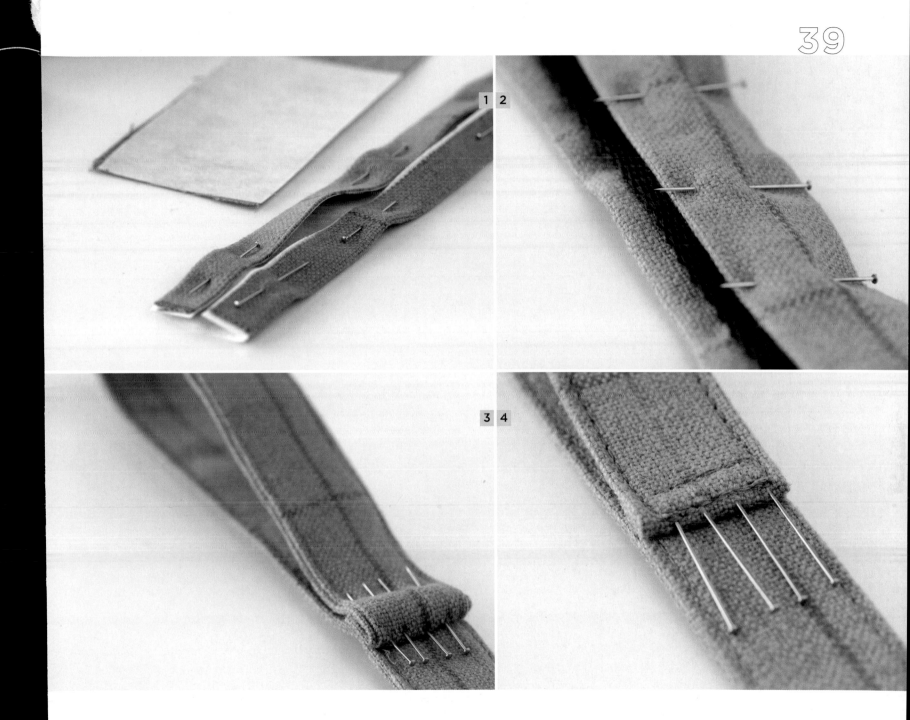

WHATEVER THE WEATHER

When you have a dog, there's no escaping the
outdoors. The two of you have to venture outside
every day, whatever the weather. Now you can
dazzle your doggy friends in the park with the
perfect coat for every season. Make the poncho
to keep him dry on wet days – he can even keep
the rain off his head with the matching
sou'wester. If it snows or if there's an icy wind,
the tweed coat will keep him snug and warm.

WINTER WOOLLIES SCARF AND LEGWARMERS

This is one of my favourite projects. It is such a lot of fun, and it doesn't matter how small or large your dog is, he or she will look just fabulous – whether the scarf and legwarmers are worn individually or as a set. Both are quick and simple to make, and can be a good way of using up oddments of leftover wool. The colours I've chosen for the stripes look fabulous on Roxy, the white standard poodle, but you can choose your own colour combination to contrast with your dog's coat and complement his or her colouring.

MATERIALS

Scarf
- 50(50:50)g any double knitting (DK) yarn, colour purple – Yarn A
- 50(50:50)g any double knitting (DK) yarn, colour orange – Yarn B
- 50(50:50)g any double knitting (DK) yarn, colour yellow – Yarn C
- 50(50:50)g any double knitting (DK) yarn, colour green – Yarn D
- Pair 4mm (UK 8) knitting needles
- 4mm (UK 8) crochet hook

Leg/ankle warmers
- 100(100:100)g any double knitting (DK) yarn, colour purple – Yarn A
- 50(50:100)g any double knitting (DK) yarn, colour orange – Yarn B
- 50(50:50)g any double knitting (DK) yarn, colour yellow – Yarn C
- 100(100:100)g any double knitting (DK) yarn, colour green – Yarn D
- Pair 4mm (UK 8) knitting needles
- 4mm (UK 8) crochet hook
- 1.5m of 12mm- or 15mm-wide soft elastic
- Sewing needle and thread
- Two safety pins

For the set
- 100(150:150)g any double knitting (DK) yarn, colour purple – Yarn A
- 100(100:150)g any double knitting (DK) yarn, colour orange – Yarn B
- 50(50:50)g any double knitting (DK) yarn, colour yellow – Yarn C
- 100(100:100)g any double knitting (DK) yarn, colour green – Yarn D

Yarn quantities are based on average requirements and are therefore approximate.

MEASUREMENTS			
SCARF	Small	Medium	Large
Width	6.5cm	9cm	9cm
Length (excluding fringe)	72cm	96cm	114cm
LEGWARMERS			
Circumference	20cm	24cm	28cm
Length	21cm	24cm	27cm

TENSION

23 sts and 30 rows = 10cm square over stocking stitch using double knitting (DK) yarn on 4mm needles or the size required to obtain the stated tension.

Always check tension carefully, and adjust needle sizes throughout if necessary.

ABBREVIATIONS

beg – beginning; **cm** – centimetres; **cont** – continue; **inc** – increase(ing); **k** – knit; **LHN** – left-hand needle; **M1K** – make one stitch by picking up the bar between the needles, then knitting into the back of it; **M1P** – make one stitch by picking up the bar between the needles, then purling into the back of it; **mm** – millimetres; **p** – purl; **patt** – pattern; **PM** – place marker; **rem** – remain(ing); **rep** – repeat; **RHN** – right-hand needle; **RS** – right side; **st-st** – stocking stitch (knit on right side rows, purl on wrong side rows); **st(s)** – stitch(es); **WS** – wrong side.
Crochet: **dc** – double crochet; **sl-st** – slip stitch.

> NOTE: When breaking and joining yarns, where appropriate leave long enough ends so that the seam can be sewn with its own colour.
> Figures in brackets ( ) refer to larger sizes. Where only one set of figures is given, this applies to all sizes.

KNITTING THE SCARF

Using 4mm needles and Yarn A, cast on 15(21:21) sts.

1st row (RS) Knit.
2nd row Purl.
Repeating 1st and 2nd rows forms stocking stitch.
Work 7 more rows in st-st, thus ending with WS facing for next row.
Break Yarn A and join Yarn B.
Beg with a WS row, work 9 rows st-st, thus ending with RS facing for next row.
Break Yarn B and join Yarn C.
Beg with a RS row, work 9 rows st-st, thus ending with WS facing for next row.
Break Yarn C and join Yarn D.
Beg with a WS row, work 9 rows st-st, thus ending with RS facing for next row.
Break Yarn D and join Yarn A.
These 36 rows form the four-colour stripe pattern.
Cont in patt until scarf measures 72(96:114)cm or length required, ending after the 9th row of a stripe.
Cast off.

BLOCKING THE SCARF

Sew ends into their own colour.
Pin the scarf to the measurements given. Press following the instructions on the skein/ball band, or cover with damp cloths and leave until dry. Stocking stitch has a natural tendency to curl towards the wrong side at the sides. Blocking the scarf as instructed will help to minimize this, but some yarns will maintain the curl more than others.

MAKING THE SCARF FRINGE

Cut 32(44:44) single strands of Yarn A, Yarn B, Yarn C and Yarn D, each 15cm long. An easy way to do this is to cut a 7.5cm square of stiff card, and wind the yarn around it 32(44:44) times. Cut the yarn along one side of the square to make strands of the correct length.
Make 16(22:22) bundles of these single strands, each bundle containing 2 strands of Yarn A, Yarn B, Yarn C and Yarn D. The cut ends of the strands should be level with each other.
Insert a 4mm crochet hook from RS to WS into the first stitch of the first row of the scarf. Fold a bundle of

strands in half to make a loop. Place the loop over the hook and draw the loop through to the RS of the scarf, then, using the hook, draw the cut ends through this loop. Remove the hook and tighten the knot just made. Tassel completed (**see picture 1**).

Make a tassel in every alternate stitch across the row to form a fringe.

Work a tassel in the first stitch of the last row of the scarf, then in every alternate stitch across the row, to form a fringe at the other end of the scarf.

KNITTING THE LEGWARMERS (MAKE 4)

Using 4mm needles and Yarn D, cast on 46(56:66) sts.
Knit 3 rows.
Break Yarn D and join Yarn A.

1st row (RS) Knit.

2nd row Purl.

Repeating 1st and 2nd rows forms stocking stitch.
Work 16 more rows in st-st, thus ending with RS facing for next row.
Break Yarn A and join Yarn B.

Forming the lower casing

1st row (RS) Fold work to WS with the join of the last row using Yarn D and the first row using Yarn A level with the LHN. K1, insert RHN into the first loop of the first row using Yarn A and lift the loop onto LHN then knit together first stitch on LHN with the loop, * insert RHN into the next loop of the first row using Yarn A and lift the loop onto LHN then knit together next stitch on LHN with the loop; rep from * to end of row. Lower casing completed (**see picture 2**).

Beg with a WS row, using Yarn B work 8 rows st-st, thus ending with WS facing for next row.
Break Yarn B and join Yarn C.
Beg with a WS row, work 9 rows st-st thus ending with RS facing for next row.
Cont in st-st and stripe sequence as follows:
9(9:9) rows Yarn D,
9(9:9) rows Yarn A,

9(9:9) rows Yarn B,
18(9:9) rows Yarn D, thus ending with WS(RS:RS) facing for next row,
0(17:9) rows Yarn A, thus ending with –(WS:WS) facing for next row,
0(0:18) rows Yarn B, thus ending with –(–:WS) facing for next row.
Break yarn leaving an end twice the width of the legwarmer. Thread this end into a wool sewing needle.

Forming the top casing

Leave sts on needle and fold work to WS, the knitting needle level with the join of the last row using Yarn B(D:A) and the first row of the 18(17:18) rows using Yarn

D(A:B). With WS facing, the point of the knitting needle should be towards the right. With WS facing, pass the threaded sewing needle from bottom to top through the first loop of the last row using Yarn B(D:A), then purlways through the first stitch of Yarn D(A:B) on the knitting needle, slipping the stitch off the knitting needle, * pass the threaded sewing needle from bottom to top through the next loop of the last row using Yarn B(D:A), then purlways through the next stitch of Yarn D(A:B) on the knitting needle, slipping the stitch off the knitting needle; repeat from * to end of row. Top casing completed (**see picture 3**).

MAKING UP THE LEGWARMERS

Sew ends not required for seaming into their own colour. Cut two 13(15:17)cm lengths of elastic.
Remove Yarn D on WS of lower casing. If the stitches have been picked up properly, then the knitting will not ladder or have any holes (**see picture 4**).
Pin the legwarmer to the measurements given. Press following the instructions on the skein/ball band, or cover with damp cloths and leave until dry.
Using mattress stitch (see right and below), starting at the edge where Yarn D was removed, join the seam on WS of lower casing and on first few rows on RS of lower casing. Thread one length of elastic through the casing. An easy way is to pin a safety pin onto one end of the elastic and secure the other end with another safety pin near to the opening in the casing. Push the first safety pin through the casing, moving the casing along the elastic until the safety pin emerges at the other end (**see picture 5**). Pin both ends of the elastic together with a 1cm overlap, then securely stitch the overlap together without twisting the elastic. Continue joining the seam on the RS, then on the first few rows of the WS of the top casing. Thread the second length of elastic through the casing and stitch, with a 1cm overlap, as before. Complete the seam (**see picture 6**).

MATTRESS STITCH NOTES FOR MAKING UP

Join the seams using yarn the same colour as the stripes. The side edge where the seaming yarn originates will be called the first side edge of the knitting and the opposite side edge will be called the second side edge.
1 Insert the needle from back (WS of knitting) to front (RS of knitting) between the first and second stitches of the first row of the second side edge of the knitting, then from back to front between the first and second cast-on stitches of the first row of the first side edge of the knitting.
2 Between each stitch is a 'bar' made by the yarn. Pick up the bar between the first and second stitch on the first row of the second side of the knitting. Then pick up the bar between the first and second stitch on the first row of the first side edge of the knitting.
3 Return to the second side edge of the knitting, and insert the needle where it came out and pick up the next bar.
4 Return to the first side of the knitting, and insert the needle where it came out and pick up the next bar.
5 Repeat steps 3 and 4. After every 2–3cm, pull the sewing yarn firmly to close the seam.

MATTRESS STITCH: Mattress stitch is worked on the right side of the knitting. When joining row edges, it is worked without the need for pinning. Usually a whole stitch is taken into the seam, and this is so when seaming the legwarmers and the collar of the sweater (on page 48). When seaming the belly to the back of the sweater, the crochet edging is taken into the seam. (The crochet edging is worked by inserting the hook into the centre of the row-edge stitch, so when the seam is sewn, only half of the knitted edge stitch will be taken into the seam with the crochet edging.)

With the right side of the knitting facing uppermost, place the row edges to be seamed side by side. Start at the cast-on edge. For the legwarmers, this will be the first row of the lower casing using Yarn A after removing the unwanted Yarn D. The seam will start on the right side of the casing, which is on the wrong side of the legwarmer. For the sweater, this will be the cast-on edge of the collar. The seaming yarn can be the end left when casting on or joining a new colour, or new yarn.

COSY STRIPY SWEATER

This sweater is wonderful for lounging around the house in the winter, as well as for wearing when you are out and about on cold days. It is snug, easy to fit and even comfy enough for your dog to sleep in. Small breeds such as Eddie the Chihuahua always love to feel warm, and a sweater like this can also be useful for keeping older dogs cosy on chilly nights. If my dog catches a cold (yes, dogs do catch colds), I always put him in a sweater to keep him wrapped up. This design has a good roll-neck, which keeps the windpipe and neck warm, as well as the chest. As always, I love using natural fibres such as wool, but you can use whatever type of yarn you like and in any colours.

MATERIALS
- 50(100:100)g any double knitting (DK) yarn, colour purple – Yarn A
- 50(50:50)g any double knitting (DK) yarn, colour lilac – Yarn B
- 50(50:50)g any double knitting (DK) yarn, colour pink – Yarn C
- 50(50:50)g any double knitting (DK) yarn, colour cream – Yarn D
- Pair 4mm (UK 8) knitting needles
- 4mm (UK 8) crochet hook
- Stitch holder
- Darning needle

Yarn quantities are based on average requirements and are therefore approximate.

COSY STRIPY SWEATER

MEASUREMENTS			
	Small	**Medium**	**Large**
Length (excluding collar)	29cm	34cm	44cm
Chest (at widest part)	35cm	41cm	44cm

NOTE: When breaking and joining yarns, where appropriate leave long enough ends so that the seam can be sewn with its own colour.

Figures in brackets ( ) refer to larger sizes. Where only one set of figures is given, this applies to all sizes.

TENSION

23 sts and 30 rows = 10cm square over stocking stitch using double knitting (DK) yarn on 4mm needles or the size required to obtain the stated tension.

Always check tension carefully, and adjust needle sizes throughout if necessary.

ABBREVIATIONS

See page 44.

SWEATER

Start at collar edge.

Using 4mm needles and Yarn A, cast on 68(80:88) sts.

1st row (RS of collar, WS of coat) * K1, p1; rep from * to end.

2nd row (WS of collar, RS of coat) *K1, p1; rep from * to end.

Repeating 1st and 2nd rows forms 1 x 1 rib.

Cont in rib until collar measures 11(11.5:11.5)cm, ending with RS of collar facing for next row.

Next row (RS of collar, WS of coat) Rib 11(15:17), M1K, rib to end. 69(81:89) sts.

Divide for Back and Belly

1st row (RS of coat) K57(65:71) sts for back of sweater, and work on these sts only. Leave rem 12(16:18) sts on a holder for belly.

2nd row Purl.

3rd row (lead hole row) (RS) K26(30:32), k1, sl 1, pass k1 over sl 1, * sl 1, pass next st on RHN over the stitch just slipped; rep from * 4(4:6) times. Slip last st on RHN back to LHN. Turn [WS facing]. Cast on 6(6:8) sts using the cable method (see page 53). Cast on 1 more stitch, bringing yarn between the needles from back to front before putting the stitch onto LHN. Turn [RS facing]. K1 and pass next st on

RHN over the k1 just worked. Knit to end. 57(65:71) sts.

4th row Purl.

Break Yarn A and join Yarn B.

Next row (RS) Knit.

Next row (WS) Purl.

Repeating last 2 rows forms stocking stitch.

Work 2 more rows st-st.

Break Yarn B and join Yarn C.

Beg with a knit row work 4 rows st-st.

Break Yarn C and join Yarn D.

Beg with a knit row work 4 rows st-st.

Breaking and joining yarns as required, cont in st-st working the stripe sequence

4 rows Yarn A,

4 rows Yarn B,

4 rows Yarn C,

4 rows Yarn D

until back of coat measures approx 26(31:41)cm from start of st-st, ending after a 4th row of a stripe and RS facing for next row.

Break current yarn and join Yarn A.

1st row (RS) Knit.

2nd row * P1, k1; rep from * to last st, p1.

3rd row K1, * p1, k1; rep from * to end.

2nd and 3rd rows form 1 x 1 rib.

Cont in rib until rib measures 3cm, ending with RS facing for next row.

Cast off in rib.

PM at each end of back between 9th and 10th(9th and 10th:12th and 13th) rows, between 34th and 35th(42nd and 43rd:49th and 50th) rows and between 45th and 46th(54th and 55th:60th and 61st) rows.

Sew ends not required for seaming into their own colour.

Belly

With RS facing, join Yarn C to 12(16:18) sts left on a holder. Beg with a knit row work 6 rows st-st.

7th row (RS) K1, M1K, knit to last 1 st, M1K, k1. 14(18:20) sts. Work 2 rows st-st.

10th row (WS) P1, M1P, purl to last st, M1P, p1. 16(20:22) sts. Cont in st-st, inc 1 st at each end of 13th, 16th, 19th, 23rd, 27th and 31st rows. 28(32:34) sts.

Cont in st-st until the 36th(46th:52nd) row has been completed from start of st-st [belly measures approximately 12(15:17)cm], thus ending with RS facing for next row.

Break Yarn C and join Yarn A.

1st row (RS) Knit.

2nd row * K1, p1; rep from * to end.

Repeating 2nd row forms 1 x 1 rib.

Cont in rib until rib measures 3cm, ending with RS facing for next row. Cast off in rib.

PM at each end of belly between 9th and 10th(9th and 10th:12th and 13th) rows and 34th and 35th(42nd and 43rd:49th and 50th) rows.

Lead hole edging

Using a 4mm crochet hook and Yarn A, with RS facing, work 1 round of edging all round lead hole as follows: Inserting hook into centre of each stitch, work 1 dc into each cast-off stitch of hole, work 1 dc at side edge of hole, work 1 dc into each cast-on stitch of hole, work 1 dc between at side edge of hole, 1 sl-st into first stitch of round. Fasten off (*see picture 1*).

Back edging

Using 4mm crochet hook and Yarn A, with RS facing, work 1 row of edging along each side edge as follows. Inserting hook into centre of row edge stitch, work 1 sl-st into each row edge stitch of the 3cm of rib, and work 1 dc into 3 out of every 4 row edge stitches of the st-st stripes. The collar does not have a crochet edging.

Belly edging

Using a 4mm crochet hook and Yarn C, with RS facing, work 1 row of edging along each side edge as follows: Inserting hook into centre of row edge stitch, work 1 dc into

3 out of every 4 row edge stitches of the st-st. The rib and the collar do not have a crochet edging.

MAKING UP THE SWEATER

Pin the sweater to the measurements given, opening out the rib of the collar and at the tail and belly. Press following the instructions on the skein/ball band, or cover with damp cloths and leave until dry. Stocking stitch has a natural tendency to curl towards the wrong side at the sides. Adding the crochet edging and blocking the sweater as instructed will help to minimize this, but some yarns will maintain the curl more than others.

With RS of collar (WS of sweater) facing, using mattress stitch (see pages 47 and 53) and Yarn A, join the collar seam for 5.5(6:6)cm, taking one stitch into the seam at each side so that the 1 x 1 rib is continuous all round. Reverse the sweater. With RS of sweater (WS of collar) facing, using mattress stitch and Yarn A, continue to join the collar seam to the end of the 1 x 1 rib, again taking one stitch into the seam at each side. Fasten off Yarn A.

Using mattress stitch and Yarn C, join the belly and back seam

1 2

3 4

from the top of the 1 x 1 rib of the collar to the marker between the 9th and 10th(9th and 10th:12th and 13th) rows [joining the 9th(9th:12th) rows ends the seam], taking the crochet edging into the seam at each side. Fasten off Yarn C (*see picture 2*). Leave the seam open between the markers at the 9th and 10th(9th and 10th:12th and 13th) rows and at the 34th and 35th(42nd and 43rd:49th and 50th) rows (*see picture 3*).

Using mattress stitch and Yarn C, join the belly and back seam, starting at the markers at the 34th and 35th(42nd and 43rd:49th and 50th) rows [joining the 35th(43rd:50th) rows starts the seam] and ending at the last row of the belly rib, matching the belly to the back row for row. Take the crochet edging into the seam at each side along the stocking stitch and half a stitch at the side edge for the belly rib.

Join the other side edge of the belly to the other side edge of the back to match.

Fold collar in half to RS of sweater.

MATTRESS STITCH NOTES FOR MAKING UP

Join seams using Yarn A for the collar and Yarn C when joining the belly and the back.

1 Starting at the cast-on edge of the RS of the collar (WS of the coat), insert the needle from back (WS of knitting) to front (RS of knitting) between the first and second stitches of the cast-on stitches of the second side edge of the knitting, then from back to front between the first and second cast-on stitches of the first side edge of the knitting, and then again from back to front between the first and second cast-on stitches of the second side edge.

2 Between each stitch is a 'bar' of yarn. Pick up the bar between the first and second stitch on the first row of the first side of the knitting. Then pick up the bar between the first and second stitch on the first row of the second side edge of the knitting.

3 Return to the first side edge of the knitting, and insert the needle where it came out and pick up the next bar.

4 Return to the second side of the knitting, and insert the needle where it came out and pick up the next bar.

CABLE CAST ON: * Insert RHN between the first 2 sts on LHN. Wrap yarn around RHN as if to knit a stitch, draw the loop through and place on LHN. One stitch cast on. Rep from *.

5 Repeat steps 3 and 4. After every 2–3cm, pull the sewing yarn firmly to close the seam. When the seam has been worked for 5.5(6:6)cm, reverse the seam so that it is worked on the WS of the collar (RS of the sweater). When the collar seam is complete, fasten off Yarn A.

6 With the RS of the sweater facing, using Yarn C continue the seam just worked to join the belly to the sweater. Insert a threaded sewing needle from back to front through the centre of the first stitch of the first row of stocking stitch on the back.

7 Insert the sewing needle from front to back through the centre of the first stitch of the first row of stocking stitch on the belly, then bring out the needle from back to front through the centre of the first stitch of the second row of stocking stitch on the belly.

8 Insert the needle from front to back where it came out of the back, then bring out the needle from back to front through the centre of the first stitch of the next row of stocking stitch on the back.

9 Insert the sewing needle from front to back where it came out of the belly, then bring out the needle from back to front through the centre of the first stitch of the next row of stocking stitch on the belly.

10 Repeat steps 8 and 9. After every 2–3cm, pull the sewing yarn firmly to close the seam. The crochet edging and half the first edge stitch should be taken into the seam.

11 Repeat the mattress stitch instructions for joining the belly and the back for the remaining belly and back seams. Only half a stitch is taken into the seam for the 3cm rib worked at the top edge of the belly.

SWISS DARN EMBROIDERY

This is an optional extra if you want to further embellish or decorate your sweater. I've put in another contrast colour against the cream to give it more of a lift. Use a yarn in a contrasting colour that's the same weight as the one you have used for the sweater. With a darning needle, just cover the underlying stitches you choose to embellish (*see picture 4*).

COUNTRY-GENT TWEED COAT

My dogs love this traditional tweed coat for weekends in the country when the weather is crisp. Short-haired breeds and older dogs, in particular, benefit from an extra layer to keep them warm in winter, and the woven tweed keeps out the chill on cold days, while the fleece lining makes this coat extra snuggly and soft to wear. Tweed is the ideal choice for a country dog – perfect for romps through the woods and fields – but you can use any wool fabric for the outer layer. Something with texture and pattern will make more of a statement, so think about your dog's colouring, and choose a fabric that will complement his markings, to ensure that he's the best-dressed hound on the hillside.

MATERIALS
- Tape measure
- Strong medium-weight paper for the pattern
- Pencil
- Scissors for paper and fabric
- Adhesive tape
- Wool fabric for the top coat
- Sherpa fleece for the lining
- Pins
- Fine fabric-marker pen
- Hook-and-loop Velcro

- Sewing machine and thread
- Medium-weight iron-on interfacing
- Iron and ironing board
- 2 belt buttons
- Needle
- Centrefold bias binding

TEMPLATES
A2, B2 and C2 for the collar, belly straps and main body.

See sizing instructions overleaf. For the belt, cut out a rectangle in pattern paper, sizing it in proportion to the rest of the coat. Fold in half lengthways, then crossways, and cut off the short ends on the diagonal to make a point on each end when opened out.

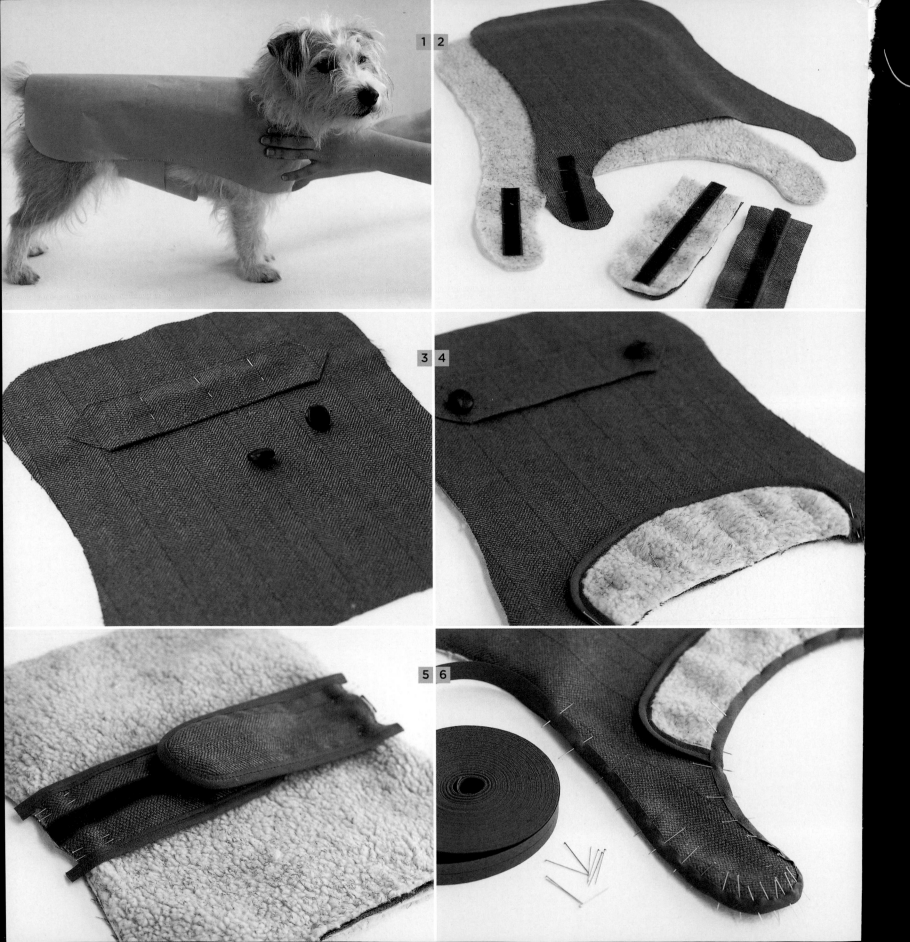

SIZING THE COAT AND CUTTING OUT THE FABRIC

Determine your dog's coat size by measuring his back from approximately 2.5cm below his collar to 5cm from his tail. Increase the template for the body of the coat on page 139 by 400 per cent, then by another 110 per cent. Then decrease or increase accordingly, so that the length of the pattern block measures the length of your dog's back. Increase the remaining sections of the pattern by the same percentage. To check the fit and work out the position for the belt and belly straps, cut out the shapes in paper and tape them together, then place the paper mock-up on your dog. Make any alterations, and mark the positions for the belt and belly straps, adjusting the length as necessary (**see picture 1**). If your dog has a long back but a small girth (like a miniature dachshund, for example), you may need to decrease the length of the paper pattern by 5–10cm to get the right fit around the neck, then lengthen the back end of the coat only; or draw around the template with a marker pen and cut off the excess areas. Once you are happy with the fit, cut out the fabric using the paper mock-up as a pattern. A 1cm seam allowance is required only for the belt piece. Cut all the pieces for the coat as follows: 1 x main body with integral neck straps (in top-coat and lining fabrics); 2 x belly straps (in top-coat and lining fabrics); 1 x belt (in top-coat fabric and iron-on interfacing); 1 x collar (in top-coat and lining fabrics).

ATTACHING THE VELCRO

Place the top coat on your dog to check where the neck straps meet under his chin. Using pins or a fabric-marker pen, mark the position for the length of Velcro you will need to fasten the straps. Cut the Velcro to length, and pin then machine-stitch one piece onto the right hand side of the neck strap (on the right side of the fabric); pin and stitch the corresponding piece onto the right-hand side of the lining (again, with the right side of the fabric facing you), making sure that the Velcro pieces are attached in the same place on the straps so that they will match up when the lining and top coat are sewn together. (The top coat and lining will be sewn together with right sides facing out, so the strips of Velcro will end up on opposing neck straps.)

For the belly straps, cut the Velcro to length, and pin then sew it centrally onto the right side of one top-coat piece and onto the right side of one lining piece (**see picture 2**).

MAKING AND ATTACHING THE BELT

Sew zigzag stitch around the top-coat belt piece to prevent fraying. Following the manufacturer's instructions, back it with iron-on interfacing. Sew a small hem around the belt. Position the belt on the back of the top-coat body piece, making sure that it is straight and central. Pin it in place, then sew a neat line from point to point down the middle of the belt to attach it (**see picture 3**). Sew the buttons onto the belt, positioning them on the central line of stitching at an equal distance from each end of the belt.

JOINING THE TOP COAT AND LINING PIECES

For each piece of the coat in turn – the main body, collar and two belly straps – place the corresponding pieces of fabric and lining together with wrong sides facing. For the belly straps, make sure that you put one top-coat piece with a Velcro strip attached to it with a lining piece without the Velcro, and vice versa. Pin around the edges of each piece, then machine-stitch.

ATTACHING THE COLLAR AND BELLY STRAPS

Pin then sew bias binding around the edge of the collar and the long U shape of the belly straps (as shown for the main body in picture 6). Place the collar centrally, fleece side up, on the front of the top coat, with the inner edge lining up with the neck of the body piece, and pin (**see picture 4**). Turn the coat over so that the fleece lining is facing up, and position the belly straps opposite each other, folded inwards with the lining sides facing down so that the Velcro meets. Line up the raw edge of the belly straps with the edge of the body piece, and pin (**see picture 5**). Sew the collar and belly straps securely to the main body

EDGING THE COAT

Conceal the raw edges of the coat with bias binding (**see picture 6**). Sew as close to the edge of the bias binding as you can, ensuring that you catch both sides in the stitching.

FISHERMAN's-FRIEND WATERPROOFS

We aren't the only ones who hate going out in the rain – lots of dogs dislike it, too. This fun poncho will brighten up those dull, grey rainy days, and keep your dog snug and dry. I chose a cotton lining fabric with a spring/summer feel, but you can use a warm fleece fabric instead, if you want to make a winter raincoat. Waterproof fabrics can be tricky to work with, so take it slowly on the sewing machine. The poncho looks fantastic on its own, so you don't have to make the matching sou'wester, but it completes this fun rainy-day outfit and will keep the rain off your dog's head. Make sure he is under close supervision when wearing it, though, and keep him on the lead.

MATERIALS
- Pins
- Tape measure
- Scissors for paper and fabric
- Iron and ironing board
- Sewing machine and thread
- Pattern paper
- Velcro
- Waterproof fabric
- Contrast cotton lining fabric
- Fabric-marker pen
- Self-cover button

TEMPLATES
C2 and B2 for the poncho. Follow the sizing instructions for the tweed coat on pages 56-7. Add a 1cm seam allowance to the pattern. B11 and C11 for the pocket and flap. Increase both parts equally as desired. Add a 1cm seam allowance. A5 and B5 for the sou'wester.

Increase the template by 400 per cent, then increase or decrease accordingly as desired. Follow the sizing instructions for the deerstalker hat on pages 72-3 to get a perfect fit. Add a 1cm seam allowance.

CUTTING OUT THE FABRICS

Using the templates on page 139, cut out a paper poncho pattern to the correct size for your dog. Cut out the following fabric pieces: 1 x main body with integral neck straps (in waterproof fabric and lining fabric); 2 x belly straps (in waterproof fabric and lining fabric). Using the templates on page 142, cut out 1 x pocket and pocket flap (in waterproof fabric and lining fabric).

MAKING UP THE BELLY STRAPS

Make up two belly straps by matching up the pieces of lining fabric and waterproof fabric, and pinning them with right sides together. Machine-stitch, leaving the straight ends at the bottom open. Turn the belly straps right side out, steam-press and topstitch along the sewn edges. Pin and sew on the Velcro strips: sew the hook Velcro onto the waterproof fabric on one belly strap and the loop Velcro onto the lining fabric on the other belly strap.

MAKING UP THE POCKET

Marry up the pocket flap pieces so that the waterproof fabric and lining fabric are right sides together. Pin and sew all around the flap, leaving one side edge open. Turn the flap right side out, tuck in the hem on the open edge, steam-press and pin. Topstitch all the way around the flap. Pin the lining and waterproof-fabric pocket pieces with right sides together (**see picture 1**). Stitch all the way around, leaving a 6cm gap on the top seam. Turn the pocket right side out, and press. Tuck in the hem at the gap, pin and topstitch the top edge only, closing the gap in the seam.

ATTACHING THE POCKET TO THE TOP COAT

Pin the main pocket piece in place on the right side of the waterproof-fabric body panel, making sure the edge that you have just topstitched is at the top. Attach the pocket to the poncho fabric by topstitching all around the two sides and bottom, leaving the top of the pocket open (**see picture 2**). Pin the pocket flap into position, so that it covers about 2.5–3cm of the top of the pocket. Topstitch along the top of the pocket flap to attach and finish the pocket (**see picture 3**).

JOINING THE WATERPROOF TOP COAT AND LINING

Marry up the lining and waterproof-fabric body panels with right sides together. Place one of the belly straps in position at one side of the poncho between the lining and waterproof-fabric body parts, sandwiching the main part of the belly strap between the two fabrics. Make sure that the belly strap is tucked in so that 1.5–2cm of the open end protrudes from the side seam of the body panel, so that the belly strap will be securely stitched into the side seam, and pin the fabrics together (**see picture 4**). Machine-stitch all the way around the body panels, leaving a gap in the other side where the final belly strap will go once the poncho has been bagged out. Bag out, steam-press and insert the final belly strap into place, carefully tucking in the hem of the body panels (**see picture 5**). Topstitch 2–3mm in all the way around the edge of the poncho.

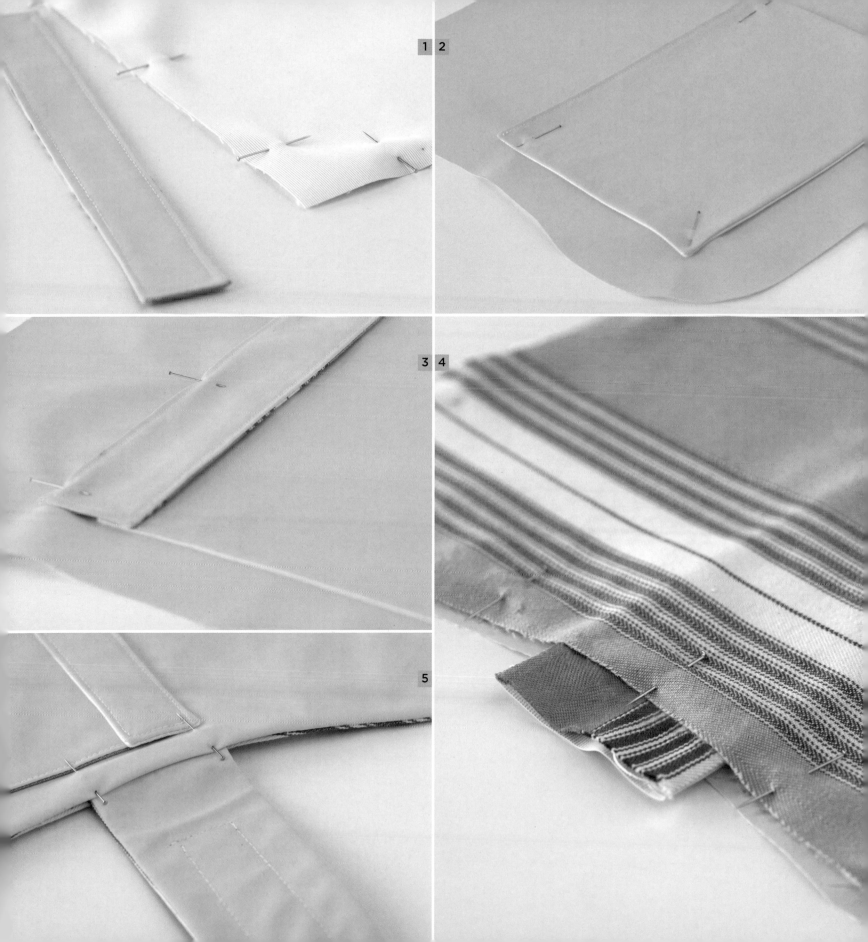

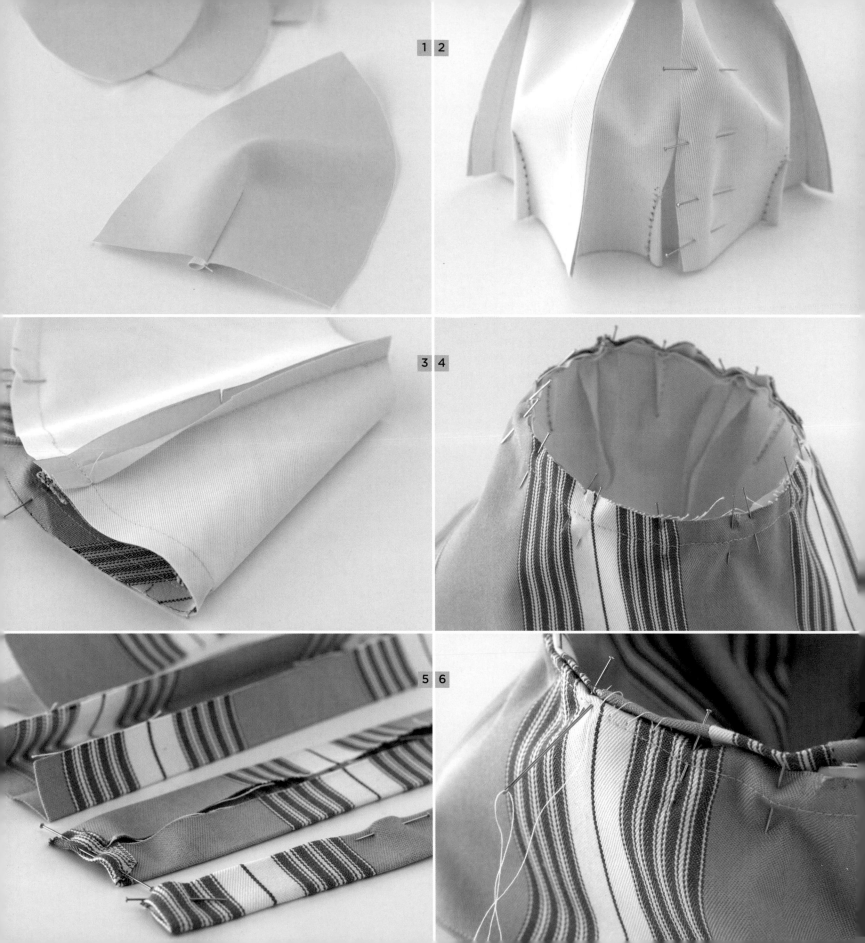

CUTTING OUT THE SOU'WESTER PIECES

Using the templates on page 143, make a paper pattern to the correct size for your dog's head, and use it to cut out the hat pieces. Cut out 6 x crown pieces in lining fabric and waterproof fabric; 1 x brim in lining and waterproof fabric. Cut 2 x 4cm-wide strips for the ties in lining fabric.

MAKING UP THE CROWN OF THE HAT

Machine-stitch a small centre pleat on each crown piece, as indicated on the pattern (*see picture 1*). Join all 6 waterproof pieces together, stitching along the sides of each, with right sides facing, to form a fan shape. Still with right sides together, join the edges of the first and sixth piece to form the crown of the hat (*see picture 2*). Repeat this process for the lining crown pieces.

MAKING UP THE BRIM OF THE HAT

Take the waterproof-fabric brim piece, and join the ends together with right sides facing. Machine-stitch along the centre back line to form a circle. Repeat for the lining. Pin the two brim pieces with right sides together, and machine-stitch along the bottom edge of the brim (*see picture 3*). Bag out the brim, and steam-press the edge for a neat finish. Machine-stitch the two layers along the crown line about 5–6mm from the raw edge. This will make it easier to sew the brim to the crown of the hat.

JOINING THE BRIM AND OUTER CROWN OF THE HAT

Pin the brim to the waterproof-fabric crown of the hat with right sides together and machine-stitch with a 1cm seam allowance, This will hide the previous stitch line that secures both layers of the brim together (*see picture 4*).

MAKING UP THE TIES

Steam-press the fabric strips in half lengthways. Fold in the long raw edges on each piece, lining them up with the centre crease, and press. Fold again to marry up the folded edges and create a long, narrow strap. Machine-stitch along the edge, 2–3mm in. To neaten the end of the ties, trim the corner on the sides that have been stitched, fold the ends in and hand-sew the edges neatly (*see picture 5*).

PINNING THE LINING AND TIES IN PLACE

Fold back the seam allowance on the lining-fabric crown, and press. This will give you a neat edge to line up with the seam at the inner edge of the brim. Place the crown lining inside the hat, and marry up the pressed edge with the stitch line on the brim; pin together. Insert the raw ends of the ties between the crown lining and the outer hat in the correct position on each side, and pin. Hand-sew the edge of the hat lining to the inner seam of the brim, catching the ends of the ties in place securely (*see picture 6*).

COVERING AND ATTACHING THE BUTTON

Cut out a circle of waterproof fabric approximately 1cm larger than the self-cover button. With a needle and thread, sew running stitch around the edge of the circle. Place the button face down on the wrong side of the fabric, and pull up the stitches to gather the fabric tightly around the button. Secure the thread with a few stitches, then sew the button onto the top of the hat.

SMART WINTER COAT

This is a great coat for any dog who needs extra warmth in the cold winter weather, but still likes to be smart. The rich red will look stunning, whatever the colouring of your dog, and will ensure that he stands out from the crowd. Being a natural fibre, the wool fabric is showerproof, as well as very warm. The check tattersall lining is also a fine 100 per cent wool fabric, which contrasts beautifully with the red melton wool top coat. Don't feel overwhelmed by the instructions – you can make the pattern simpler by omitting the collar and just having a round neck. You can also create your own style of pocket or belt band – you don't have to do exactly the same as the pattern.

MATERIALS
- Pattern paper and sticky tape
- Tape measure
- Fabric-marker pen
- Scissors for paper and fabric
- Wool fabric for the coat
- Contrast lining fabric
- Pins
- Sewing machine and thread
- Iron and ironing board
- Hook-and-loop Velcro
- 6 buttons

TEMPLATES
C2 and B2 for the body and belly straps. Follow the sizing instructions for the tweed coat on pages 56–7. See overleaf for instructions regarding the pleat.
A11 for the pocket flap. Increase or decrease this to the desired size. You will also need to cut a square shape to match the pocket flap width.

Add a 1cm seam allowance. A1, B1, C1 and D1 for the belt, collar, stand, fall and peak. Increase by 200 per cent, then decrease or increase accordingly to match the size of your coat pattern. Make a paper mock-up of the collar pattern first, and make any necessary adjustments to get a good fit. Add a 1cm seam allowance.

CUTTING OUT THE FABRICS

Using the templates on pages 139, 140 and 142, and referring to the instructions on sizing on pages 56–7, cut out a paper coat pattern to the correct size for your dog. You will need to add 15–20cm to the width of the coat (between the neck straps) to allow for the pleat. To check this is accurate, once you are happy with the size of your paper pattern, cut it in half through the centre, from the middle of the neck down to the hem. Cut out a paper rectangle 15–20cm wide and the length of your coat, and tape it in between the two halves of your coat pattern. When you are happy with the width of the pleat, mark notches for its centre and fold lines. Cut out all the fabric pieces: 1 x main coat body with integral neck straps (in main fabric and lining fabric); 2 x belly straps (in main fabric and lining fabric); 2 x pockets and pocket flaps (in main fabric and lining fabric); 1 x collar stand (in main fabric and lining fabric); 2 x collar fall (in main fabric); 4 x collar peak (in main fabric); 1 x belt (in main fabric and lining fabric). Make a small snip in the fabric to mark the notches indicated on the pattern.

MAKING UP THE COLLAR

Marry up the collar fall pieces with right sides together, and machine-stitch along the two sides and the top. Trim back the seam allowance, and trim off the excess in the corners, creating a V shape – don't cut too close to the stitch line (no closer than 2mm at the corners). Turn the fabric through to the right side, and steam-press, making sure the points are neatly pushed out. Topstitch the collar on the three outer sides, but not the edge that will be attached to the coat neckline (**see picture 1**).

Marry up the front panel of the collar stand with the front panel of the collar fall, matching up the notches and with right sides together. Do the same for the back panels. With all four layers pinned together, machine-stitch them securely (**see picture 2**). Then, separating the collar stand layers from the collar fall, press flat, making sure you fold back the seam allowance on the ends of the collar stand as you do so.

To make up the collar peaks, marry up the front collar peak pieces, and machine-stitch them together along the outer edge and the side edge up to the notch mark. Trim away the excess seam allowance, and snip back the corner to create a neat V shape. Carefully make a cut along your notch line up to the stitch line (**see picture 3**). Turn the collar peak right side out, carefully pushing out the point and the seam allowance beyond the notch mark on the side seam. Steam-press flat, and topstitch the outside edge and side edge, 2–3mm in, up to the notch mark.

Attach one collar peak to each end of the collar stand by inserting the small section of seam allowance protruding from the side edge of the collar peaks between the pressed-back collar-stand ends. Pin in place, and topstitch securely (**see picture 4**).

MAKING UP THE POCKETS

Marry up the front pocket panels with the lining pocket panels with right sides together, and pin. Do the same for the pocket flaps. Machine-stitch along both sides and the bottom, leaving the top edges on both the pockets and the flaps unstitched. Trim away the excess seam allowance, and snip the corners into V shapes. Turn the pockets and flaps right sides out and steam-press flat. Fold back the seam allowance on the raw edges of the top of the pockets and flaps, and pin them securely.

Pin both pockets onto the outer-fabric panel of the coat, positioning them according to the pattern guides. Topstitch the sides and bottom of the pockets to secure them in place on the coat body. Place the pocket flaps directly above the pocket and, where you have pinned the seam allowances back on the top edge of the flap, topstitch them onto the coat panel, sealing off the flap and securing it to the body of the coat as you do so.

ATTACHING THE VELCRO

Sew the Velcro pieces for the neck fastening in place on the front panel of the coat and its lining. Attach one piece to the right side of the lining on the left neck strap and the corresponding piece to the right side of the top coat on the right neck strap. Before you sew them in place, double-check that the Velcro pieces are positioned on the right side of each neck strap.

MAKING UP THE BELLY STRAPS

Sew one strip of Velcro onto a lining piece, then sew the corresponding strip of Velcro onto an outer-fabric piece. Marry up the lining piece with the Velcro to the outer-fabric piece without the Velcro. Machine-stitch all the way around the edges, leaving the straight section at the bottom unstitched (this will be attached to the coat later). Trim the seam allowance, then turn right side out, steam-press and topstitch the edge to finish off the strap. Repeat for the second belly strap.

Attach the belly straps onto the outer-fabric coat panel, positioning them according to the notches shown on the pattern. It helps if you put in a few more pins along the length of the strap, so that it doesn't move around as you sew up the coat body.

JOINING THE OUTER FABRIC BODY PANEL TO THE LINING

Pin the outer-fabric coat panel to the lining panel with right sides together. Machine-stitch around the edge of the coat, leaving the neckline open. Trim the excess seam allowance, and cut some notches along the curved edges – this will help to prevent wrinkles when you turn the coat through to the right side.

Turn the coat right side out, and steam-press flat, then topstitch all the way around the edge, still leaving the neckline unstitched. Remove the extra pins that are holding the belly straps in place.

CREATING THE PLEAT

Following the notch marks, bring the coat together at the centre to form the pleat, and pin it in place at the neckline and the waistline (**see picture 5**). Topstitch securely in a straight line across the pleat to keep it in place (**see picture 6**). The belt will cover the top-stitched line at the waist, while the collar will hide the one at the neckline.

ATTACHING THE COLLAR TO THE COAT BODY

Marry up the seam allowance on the lining side of your collar with the seam allowance on the lining side of the coat neckline, pin and sew together. Trim away the excess seam allowance and make a few notches along the curved neckline to help prevent wrinkles and creases around the neck area. Fold the seam allowance into the coat body, and lay the collar and coat body flat. Carefully make some notches along the outer-fabric coat neckline, then fold back into the coat and pin to the collar. Topstitch all the layers together securely along the neckline about 3mm from the edge.

MAKING AND ATTACHING THE BELT

Pin the lining and outer fabric belt pieces with right sides together, and machine-stitch all the way around, leaving a gap of approximately 6cm for turning the belt through to the right side. Trim away the excess

seam allowance, and make some notches on the curved ends. Turn the belt through to the right side, and steam-press flat, then topstitch all the way around approximately 5mm from the edge. Finish off the belt by sewing a button on at either end of the strap (see below). Use this opportunity to hand-sew the remaining buttons onto the coat pockets and collar.

Pin the belt onto the back of the coat, positioning it centrally and making sure that it is straight. Hand-sew or machine-stitch it in place. You can either sew a line down the middle of the belt's length, from one end to the other, or stitch it down at either end, following the lines of topstitching around the curved ends.

70 DEERSTALKER HAT

If you are making the Country-Gent Tweed Coat (on page 54), you just have to complete the outfit and make this deerstalker hat to go with it. Together, they make the perfect costume for a weekend in the country and will ensure that your dog looks the part, whether you're hunting, shooting or fishing, or just plain rambling. This hat is a favourite with long-eared breeds, such as cocker spaniels, as it prevents their ear fur from getting tangled in the wind when enjoying the great outdoors. You don't need great sewing skills to make this hat – it's easier than it looks – and you can use the template for the hat's crown, then create your own style of hat by changing the shape of the brim and ear flaps.

MATERIALS
- Pattern paper
- Adhesive tape
- Tape measure
- Pencil or fabric-marker pen
- Scissors for paper and fabric
- 100 per cent wool tweed fabric for the hat
- Contrasting cotton fabric for the lining
- Pins
- Sewing machine and thread
- Two 1m lengths of ribbon for the ties
- Iron and ironing board
- String (for measuring)

TEMPLATES
A4, B4, C4 and D4. Increase the pattern templates on page 142 by 230 per cent, then increase or decrease them by 13 per cent to achieve the correct size for your dog. To get a perfect fit, measure the crown of your dog's head where you want the hat to sit, then divide this measurement by six to give you the approximate width that each A4 template should measure along the bottom (this is the base of the triangle shape of A4). Adjust the size of all the other template parts to match.

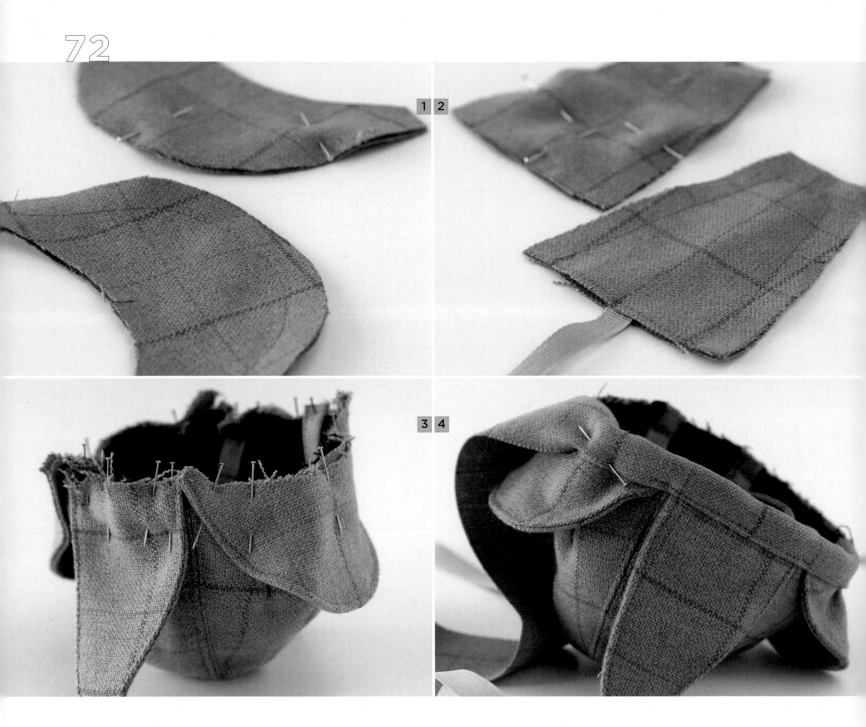

1 2

3 4

CUTTING OUT THE FABRIC

Using the template on page 142, make a paper pattern to the correct size for your dog's head, and use it to cut out all the hat pieces. Cut out 6 x crown pieces in cotton lining fabric and wool outer fabric; 1 x front and 1 x rear flap pieces in lining and outer fabric; 2 x ear flaps in lining and outer fabric; 1 x binding strip in outer fabric.

MAKING UP THE CROWN OF THE HAT

Referring also to the instructions for the sou'wester on pages 62–3, machine-stitch a small centre pleat on each crown piece, as marked on the pattern. With right sides together, stitch all 6 wool crown pieces together along the side seams to form a fan shape. Still with right sides together, join the side of the first piece to the side of the sixth piece to form the crown of the hat. Repeat this process to make up the lining of the hat.

MAKING UP THE FLAPS

Marry up the outer fabric and lining of the front and rear flaps with right sides together, and pin. Machine-stitch around the outside curve only (*see picture 1*).

Do the same for the side ear flaps, this time inserting the ribbon ties so that they are sandwiched centrally between the two layers of fabric and stitched into the seam at the narrowest end. When the flaps are turned right side out, the ribbon will hang from the bottom end of the side flaps (*see picture 2*). Hem the raw end of the ribbon.

Trim the seam allowances, and turn the four flaps right side out. Steam-press to make sure you get crisp lines along the sewn edges.

LINING THE HAT

Place the lining piece into the outer-fabric crown with wrong sides facing, and pin together. Machine-stitch around the raw edge, securing both layers together.

ATTACHING THE FLAPS

Pin the side flaps and the front and back flaps into place around the brim of the hat, according to the notches shown on the pattern (*see picture 3*). Machine-stitch all the layers securely together.

MEASURING THE CORRECT LENGTH FOR THE EAR LOOPS

Cut a length of string or use a tape measure, and measure from under your dog's chin up the side of his head to the crown of his head, directly above his ear. This gives you the approximate length to cut the tie for the ear loops. Add a 1cm seam allowance to each end of this measurement.

MAKING UP THE EAR LOOPS AND HAT TIE

Cut two lengths of wool fabric, approximately 50cm long and 4cm wide. Fold each one in half lengthways, steam-press, and fold the raw edges into the centre to the fold line. Fold each one in half again, and topstitch along the edge, 2–3mm in, securing the two folded edges together.

Cut off two short strands to make up the ear loops, according to your measurement (see above), and use the remainder for the tie. Pin the two short strands in place on the brim of the hat, positioning them to the right and left of each ear flap, and topstitch in place.

EDGING THE HAT

Finish by neatly folding and pinning the binding strip along the raw edge of the brim, and topstitch in place (*see picture 4*). Loop the remaining tie through the ear loops and tie off in a knot, cutting any excess off after trying it on your dog and pulling tight to fit.

NOTE: Always supervise your dog when he is wearing a hat, and keep him on the lead.

DEERSTALKER HAT

HIGH DAYS & HOLIDAYS

Everyone loves a party, whether it's to

celebrate a birthday or Christmas, or just a

gathering of friends and family – so why should

your dog miss out? She can join in the fun, too,

and be the belle of the ball in the pink velvet

party dress, feel special in her own birthday

T-shirt while blowing out the candles

on her cake, or just look gorgeous in a

festive bandana, guarding the presents

under the Christmas tree.

FESTIVE GIFT STOCKING

In our house, everyone gets a present at Christmas, including our dogs. They are part of the family, and we don't want to leave them out. Try to plan ahead, so you can eliminate the stress and make sure Christmas is an enjoyable experience for you, your family and, of course, your beloved four-legged friend. He has been a loyal companion to you all year, so he deserves a treat at Christmas. This festive stocking can be stuffed full of healthy biscuits, favourite chews and new fun toys for him to play with (see page 18), or a new bandana to wear on Christmas Day (see page 80). This project is a great way to use up any leftover fabrics, and it adds a lovely festive touch to your home.

MATERIALS
- Pattern paper
- Fabric-marker pen
- Tape measure
- Scissors for paper and fabric
- Fabric for the stocking panel
- Fabric for the contrasting cuff panel
- Sewing machine and thread
- Pins
- Iron, ironing board and ironing cloth
- Tracing paper
- Thin card for templates
- Fabric scraps for the appliqué decoration
- Iron-on adhesive
- Backing paper for the appliqué
- 20cm of cotton cord or string for the loop

TEMPLATES
A9 and B9.
Increase your template to the desired size. Add a 1cm seam allowance.

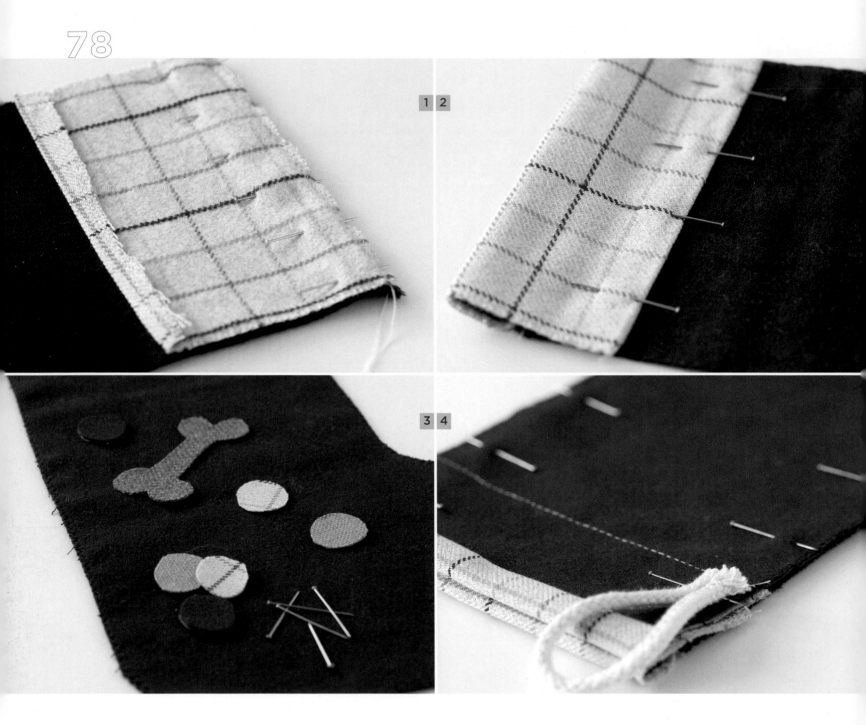

CUTTING OUT THE FABRIC

Using the templates on page 139, cut out the following: 2 x stocking shape in the main wool fabric and 2 x stocking cuff in the contrasting wool fabric. Cut the required length of cotton cord or string for the hanging loop – approximately 20cm is ideal. Overlock or zigzag-stitch around the edges of all the stocking pieces to make your stocking harder-wearing.

ATTACHING THE CUFF

Pin one of the cuff panels to one of the main stocking panels, with the right side of the cuff facing the wrong side of the stocking. Align the top edges, and machine-stitch with a 1cm hem allowance. Turn up a 1cm hem along the bottom edge of the cuff, and press in place (***see picture 1***). Flip the cuff over, and pin the bottom edge into place along the front of the stocking panel. Machine-stitch it down, sewing 2–3mm from the folded edge of the cuff (***see picture 2***). Repeat for the other stocking and cuff pieces.

CREATING THE APPLIQUÉ MOTIFS

Choose the decorative motifs you would like to use for the appliqué (see page 138), and make card templates of these. Following the method described for the Tidy-Toys Bag on page 18, back your appliqué fabrics with iron-on adhesive, and cut out the motifs. I used a mixture of spots, hearts and bones.

ATTACHING THE APPLIQUÉ MOTIFS

Arrange the motifs on the right side of the front stocking panel, making sure there are 2–3cm clear between them and the edge of the fabric (***see picture 3***). Referring again to the instructions on page 18, peel off the backing and iron the motifs onto the fabric to fuse them in place, then machine-stitch around the edges of the motifs using satin stitch.

MAKING UP THE STOCKING

Fold the piece of cord in half, and pin the loop into position at the top of the outside edge of one of the stocking pieces, on the wrong side of the fabric and with the cut ends facing down. Stitch across the ends of the cord to hold it in place, about 1cm up from the cut ends. Place the front and back panels of the stocking together with right sides facing. Make sure the edges are aligning neatly, and pin into place (***see picture 4***). Using a seam allowance of 1cm, machine-stitch down one side of the stocking, around the foot and up the other side. Turn the stocking right side out, and press for a neat finish.

SNAZZY BANDANA

Traditional bandanas are lovely accessories for dogs of all sizes, whatever the season. They can be worn very stylishly both indoors and out, tied simply at one side of the neck. Holly the chocolate Labrador looks splendid in her cheery winter bandana, made in festive colours and decorated with a smattering of snowballs. Bandanas are very easy and quick to make, and they are the ideal way to use up odd ends of fabric, as you need only a small quantity. You could make a whole wardrobe of bandanas for your dog to wear in the spring, summer, autumn and winter, using different colours and patterns, and decorating them with different appliqué motifs.

MATERIALS
- Tape measure
- Pattern paper
- Fabric-marker pen
- Scissors for paper and fabric
- Velvet fabric
- Red-and-white cotton gingham check
- Tracing paper
- Thin card for templates
- Red felt and cream cotton fabric for the appliqué
- Iron-on adhesive
- Iron and ironing board
- Pins
- Sewing machine and thread

SIZING THE BANDANA AND CUTTING OUT THE FABRIC

Measure your dog's neck, and add an extra 10–15cm onto each end of that measurement, allowing enough excess to enable you to tie a good, secure knot in the finished bandana. Draw a line this length onto your pattern paper, and form a triangle with a depth that is roughly a third of the length. Do this by drawing a perpendicular line from the centre of the first line to form the tip of the triangle, then join this to each end of your first line with a diagonal line. Add a 1cm seam allowance all around, and cut out the paper pattern. Next, cut out one bandana shape in velvet and one in gingham check.

CREATING THE APPLIQUÉ MOTIFS

Make card templates of the dog and spot shapes on page 138. Following the method described for the Tidy-Toys Bag on page 18, back the red felt and cream cotton appliqué fabrics with iron-on adhesive, and cut

out sufficient red dog and cream snowball motifs to decorate your bandana.

ATTACHING THE APPLIQUÉ MOTIFS

Arrange the red felt dog shapes along the long edge of the gingham check, making sure that the dogs' feet are approximately 1.5cm from the long edge, so that they will be the correct way up when the gingham edge is turned over as you tie the bandana in place (**see picture 1**). Referring again to the instructions on page 18, peel off the backing, and iron the motifs onto the fabric to fuse them in place, then machine-stitch around the edges of the motifs using satin stitch.

Arrange the snowball shapes randomly on the velvet triangle, and appliqué them in the same way.

MAKING UP THE BANDANA

Place both fabrics with right sides together, marrying up the outlines of the triangles, and pin in place (**see picture 2**). Stitch all the way around, leaving a gap of 6–8cm in the centre of the long edge for turning the bandana through.

Turn the bandana right side out and press the seams, folding in the hem at the gap in the seam. Topstitch the long edge of the bandana 2–3mm in from the edge to close the gap (**see picture 3**). Finally, trim any stray threads and press to finish so that the appliqué shapes lie flat (**see picture 4**).

1 2

3 4

SNAZZY BANDANA

84

PINK PARTY DRESS

Dogs are pack animals and love being sociable as much as you do. So let your dog join in the festivities and dress up for a special occasion, whether it's for a friend's birthday or just a night of fun. This pretty party dress is a pleasure to make, as you can really go to town with your choice of embellishments. Experiment with different textures and colours, and add an element of sparkle for extra glamour. Choose textures and shades that will complement your dog's colouring – I used strong, contrasting colours to suit Daisy the miniature dachshund – remember that this is a fashion coat for a special occasion and not for everyday wear: she should be the belle of the ball.

MATERIALS
- Pattern paper
- Tape measure
- Fabric-marker pen
- Scissors for paper and fabric
- Adhesive tape
- Velvet fabric for the top coat
- Contrast Liberty-print cotton fabric for the lining
- Pins
- Hook-and-loop Velcro
- Sewing machine and thread

- Silk flowers with wire stems
- Needle
- Satin centrefold bias binding
- Decorative metallic belt
- Iron and ironing board

TEMPLATES
C2 and B2.
Follow the sizing instructions for the tweed coat on pages 56–7, leaving out the collar.

CUTTING OUT THE COAT

Using the coat template on page 139 and referring to the instructions for the Country-Gent Tweed Coat on page 57, make a paper pattern to fit your dog and use this to cut out the fabric as follows: 1 x main body with integral neck straps (in top-coat and lining fabrics); 2 x belly straps (in top-coat and lining fabrics).

ATTACHING THE VELCRO

Place the top coat loosely over your dog to check where the neck straps meet under his chin. Using a couple of pins or a fabric-marker pen, mark the position for the length of Velcro you will need to fasten the straps. Cut the Velcro to length; pin then machine-stitch one piece onto the right-hand side of the neck strap (on the right side of the fabric), then pin and stitch the corresponding piece onto the right-hand side of the lining (again, with the right side of the fabric facing you), making sure that the Velcro pieces are attached in the same place on the straps, so that they'll match up when the lining and top coat are sewn together. (The top coat and lining will be sewn together with right sides facing out, so the strips of Velcro will end up on opposing neck straps.) For the belly straps, cut the Velcro to length; pin then sew it centrally onto the right side of one top-coat piece and onto the right side of one lining piece (*see picture 1*).

ATTACHING THE FLOWERS TO THE NECKLINE

Overlock or zigzag-stitch the neckline of the velvet top coat to prevent the fabric from fraying. Arrange the stems of the flowers along the neckline, to make sure you have enough to make a substantial 'collar' with no large gaps in between the flowers. Mark each stem placement with a pin, then remove the flowers. Bend the wire stem of the first flower back gently, so that it hooks over the edge of the fabric and underneath. Carefully hand-sew the stem to the velvet fabric, securing it in place approximately 1cm in from the edge of the neckline. Repeat for the rest of the flowers, then cut off the excess wire stems, leaving a length of about 2cm on the underside of the velvet (*see picture 2*).

ATTACHING THE BELT

Cut two lengths of bias binding, and loop them through the belt buckles. Pin the ends of the bias binding on either side of the velvet top coat, at the point where the belly straps will go (*see pictures 3 and 4*). Machine-stitch the belt in place on the edges of the coat and close to the buckles.

MAKING UP THE COAT

Referring to the instructions on page 57, pin and machine-stitch the top coat and lining together with wrong sides facing (*see picture 5*). Marry up the belly straps, putting one top-coat piece with a Velcro strip attached to it with the lining piece without Velcro, and vice versa. Pin then machine-stitch bias binding around the U shape of the belly straps. Pin then sew the belly straps in place on the coat, then edge the coat with the satin bias binding and machine-stitch. (*see picture 6*). Lightly press on the inside.

PINK PARTY DRESS

BIRTHDAY T-SHIRT AND CAKE

I love my dog's birthday – it's the best excuse to celebrate my love for him. I always have a party for him, and some of his canine friends come, too. Even if my dog lives a happy, healthy and full life, he won't outlive me, so I want to make the most of his life and enjoy every single year that I am lucky enough to have with him. Make your dog's day extra special by making a birthday T-shirt – like Pippa's, which has a large number 2 to mark her second birthday. You can even bake a cake as a special treat that you can all enjoy – but only give your dog one small portion. Your dog may not really know what is going on, but he or she will enjoy all the excitement and being fussed over.

MATERIALS
- Pattern paper
- Fabric-marker pen
- Scissors for paper, fabric and appliqué
- Cotton jersey fabric in three colours (one for the back, one for the front and collar, one for the sleeves and motif)
- Tracing paper and pencil
- Thin card for template
- Pins and safety pin
- Sewing machine and thread
- Waistband elastic, 1cm wide

For the cake
- 225g self-raising flour
- 120g runny honey
- 50g chopped pecans
- 100g grated carrots
- 2 sliced bananas
- 2 eggs
- 150ml sunflower oil
- Cream cheese, to decorate

TEMPLATES
A10, B10, C10 and D10. Increase the templates by 200 per cent, then increase or decrease them accordingly to fit your dog. Your A10 template should measure the length of your dog's back. (See the sizing instructions for the tweed coat on pages 56–7). Add a 1cm seam allowance.

CUTTING OUT THE FABRIC

Using the templates on page 143, cut out all the pieces of cotton jersey fabric as follows: 1 x back piece in dark blue; 1 x front piece in turquoise; 1 x collar in turquoise; 2 x sleeves in orange.

CREATING AND ATTACHING THE APPLIQUÉ MOTIF

Appliqué the number onto the back panel before sewing the garment together, as it will be easier to do this when the fabric is still flat. Make a card template of one of the numbers on page 138, enlarged to the desired size. Choose jersey fabric in a contrasting colour to the back panel piece, and trace the number onto the right side using a fabric-marker pen. Draw a square approximately 2cm outside the number, and cut it out. Position the square centrally on the back panel of the T-shirt, and pin into place. Zigzag-stitch around the outline of the number, then cut away the excess fabric outside the stitched outline using appliqué scissors.

MAKING UP THE T-SHIRT

Pin the front and back panels of the T-shirt together with right sides facing. Using a 1cm seam allowance, machine-stitch along the shoulder seams and the side seams to join the front and back panels (*see picture 1*).

Make up the sleeves by pinning and machine-stitching along the inside seams, with right sides together and a 1cm seam allowance (*see picture 2*). Then, with right sides together, insert the sleeves into the T-shirt body, and machine-stitch around the shoulder seams (*see picture 3*). Hem the bottom edges of the sleeves and T-shirt by folding the edges over twice and topstitching them down.

Fold the collar piece in half; pin then machine-stitch it around the neckline of the T-shirt, with the seam on the inside. Leave an opening at the back, and use a safety pin to thread the elastic through the neck binding. Machine-stitch the ends together using zigzag stitch (*see picture 4*).

CAKE RECIPE

1 Preheat the oven to 180°C/350°F/gas mark 4. Grease a 20cm round cake tin, and line the bottom with greaseproof paper or baking parchment.

2 Put the flour, honey, chopped pecans, grated carrot, sliced bananas, eggs and oil in a mixing bowl or food processor, and beat well. Pour the mixture into the cake tin, and bake for 50–60 minutes until springy to the touch.

3 Let the cake cool in the tin for a few minutes, then turn out onto a wire rack and leave to cool completely.

4 Spread a thin layer of cream cheese on top of the cake, and decorate it with candles and pecan halves.

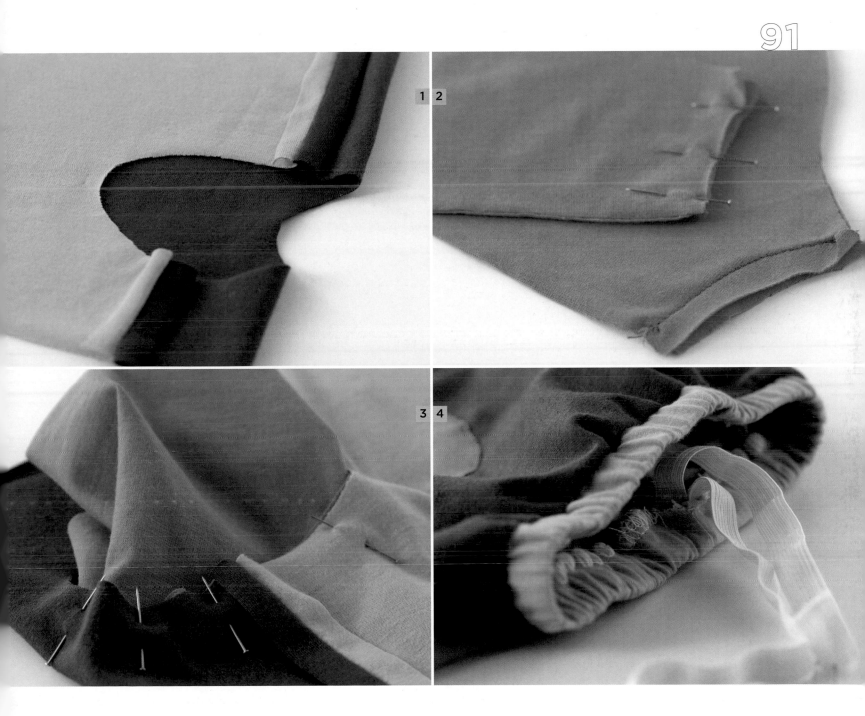

BIRTHDAY T-SHIRT AND CAKE

VELVET SMOKING JACKET

Your dog should look as good as you do on a special occasion, and there's no reason for your butch little boy to miss out on the party outfits. This dashing velvet smoking jacket makes a great boy's equivalent to the Pink Party Dress on page 84. It is also lined with Liberty-print cotton, but has a smart wide collar and pocket instead of the flower ruffle and sparkly belt. You could make the pair in toning colours for a matching his-and-hers look. You don't need to splash out a fortune to treat your dog to a new party coat, but you can still use luxurious fabrics, such as velvet, to make him look dapper, and trim his party coat with satin bias binding in a contrasting or toning colour.

MATERIALS
- Pattern paper
- Fabric-marker pen
- Tape measure
- Scissors for paper and fabric
- Adhesive tape
- Pins
- Velvet fabric for the top coat
- Contrast Liberty-print cotton fabric for the lining
- Hook-and-loop Velcro
- Sewing machine and thread
- Iron and ironing board
- Satin centrefold bias binding
- Needle

TEMPLATES
C2 and B2 for the coat body and belly straps. Follow the sizing instructions for the tweed coat on pages 56–7. E3 for the pocket. Increase in size as desired. Add a 1cm seam allowance all around. B1 and C1 for the collar and collar stand. Increase the templates by 200 per cent, then increase or decrease accordingly to match your coat body pattern (see overleaf). Add a 1cm seam allowance for the collar and stand.

VELVET SMOKING JACKET

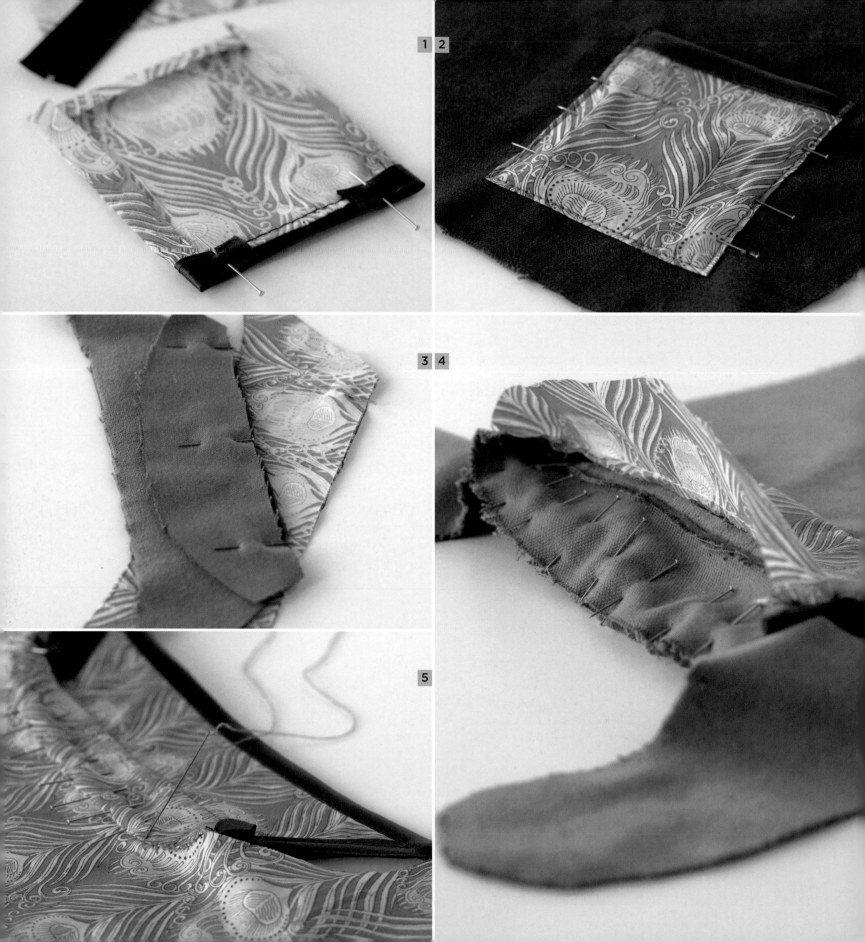

CUTTING OUT THE COAT PIECES

Using the coat template on page 139 and referring to the instructions for the Country-Gent Tweed Coat on page 57, make a paper mock-up to fit your dog and use this pattern to cut out the fabric as follows: 1 x main body with integral neck straps (in top-coat and lining fabrics); 2 x belly straps (in top-coat and lining fabrics).

Make a paper pattern for the pocket using the template for the bathrobe on page 141 – you can make it larger or smaller, as you wish. Cut out the pocket square in lining fabric.

Using the template for the winter coat on page 140, cut out the collar and stand in both velvet and lining fabric.

ATTACHING THE VELCRO

Follow the instructions for the Pink Party Dress on page 87 to sew Velcro onto the neck and belly straps.

MAKING AND ATTACHING THE POCKET

Press a 1cm hem along each edge of the pocket piece, and machine-stitch along the top edge. Pin the centrefold bias binding along the top edge of the pocket, on the right side of the fabric, and flip the ends over to the inside of the pocket. Machine-stitch the satin trimming to the top of the pocket (*see picture 1*). Pin the pocket centrally onto the top coat, and machine-stitch along the sides and bottom, 2–3mm in from the edge, to secure it in place (*see picture 2*).

MAKING THE COLLAR

With right sides together, pin then machine-stitch the collar to the stand for both fabrics, and press the seams open (*see picture 3*). Next, pin the two fabrics together with right sides facing. Using a 1cm seam allowance, machine-stitch all around the outer sides, leaving the stand end of the collar open to attach the collar to the neckline of the coat later. Turn the fabrics right side out, and press.

PREPARING THE BELLY STRAPS

Referring to the instructions for the tweed coat on page 57, make up the two belly straps, and edge them with satin bias binding around the U shape.

MAKING UP THE COAT

With right sides together, align the edge of the velvet collar stand with the neckline of the velvet top coat, and pin in place (*see picture 4*). Machine-stitch, and press from the wrong side of the velvet collar stand.

Pin bias binding around the collar, stopping just before the start of the stand and leaving plenty of excess at each end to join up with the bias binding around the body of the coat later. Machine-stitch in place. Turn under a 1cm hem on the lining of the collar stand and press.

With wrong sides facing, pin the lining and top coat together, inserting the belly straps between them on either side. Machine-stitch all the way around the edge of the coat, stopping at the start and finish of the collar stand. Pin the hem of the collar stand onto the lining of the coat neckline, and slipstitch it to the lining (*see picture 5*).

Pin and machine-stitch bias binding around the edge of the coat, carefully folding over the excess collar bias binding when it meets up with the main body bias.

VELVET SMOKING JACKET

JET-SETTING KIT

Gone are the days when Fido was left
at home. Now you can take your dog on
holiday with you, and he can have all his creature
comforts. When you get the overnight bag out,
your dog will know he is going somewhere
special. The travel blanket is light and easy to
pack; the safari jacket is perfect for any trip; and
if you fancy a picnic on a sunny day, don't let him
go without water and a comfy rug to snooze on –
you can even make a matching ball.

OVERNIGHT BAG

I made this overnight bag for Rabbit, for when he goes away on short breaks with me or on sleepovers with friends or family. It's simple to make, lightweight, washable and practical; the strap is long enough to put across my shoulder and leave both hands free, while the extra-large flap instead of a fastening means that I can get into it easily. Here's what I pack for Rabbit's weekend breaks: a roll-up travel blanket (page 104); a warm sweater in case it's cold (page 48); his favourite toy – especially important if he's going to an unfamiliar place (page 26); a supply of dog food; his towel and grooming brush to wipe and brush mud off; a travel bowl for the journey and days out; and a spare collar and lead (page 34).

MATERIALS

- Tape measure
- Fabric-marker pen
- 1m lightweight cotton twill for the outer fabric
- 1m contrast or patterned cotton fabric for the lining
- Scissors for fabric and paper
- Tracing paper
- Sharp pencil
- Thin card for template
- Fabric scraps for the appliqué motifs
- Iron-on adhesive
- Iron, ironing board and ironing cloth
- Pins
- Sewing machine and thread
- 1m webbing/strapping for the shoulder strap

OVERNIGHT BAG

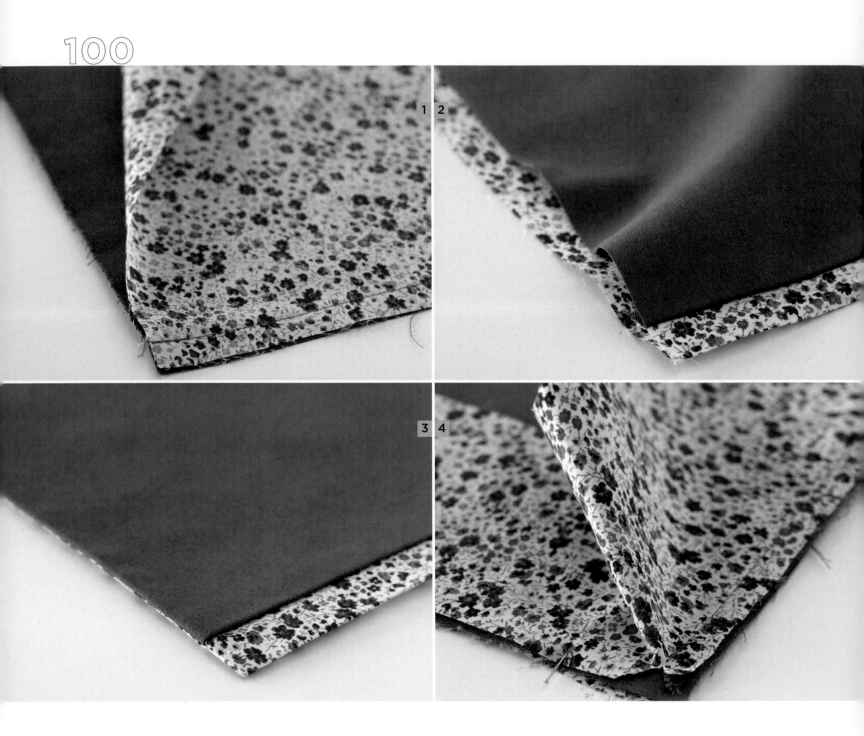

JET-SETTING KIT

CUTTING OUT THE FABRIC

Measure and cut out the following pieces: 2 x panels for the front and back in main fabric and in lining fabric, 40 x 34cm; 1 x front flap in main fabric, 38 x 30cm; 1 x front flap lining in lining fabric, 38 x 34cm; 1 x centre panel (or gusset) in main fabric and lining fabric – cut this on the fold with a length of 54cm and a width of 11cm tapering to 6.5cm (keep straight for the first 20cm down from the fold, then taper to make the narrower width of 6.5cm at the end).

CREATING THE APPLIQUÉ MOTIFS

Choose the appliqué motifs you would like to use to decorate the front bag panel and flap (see page 138). I used a bone shape for the front bag panel, and a heart, circle and initial on the bag flap. Using tracing paper and a pencil, trace around the motifs, then transfer them onto thin card to make a template. Cut out the shapes using paper scissors. Following the manufacturer's instructions, back your appliqué fabric with iron-on adhesive. Place the card motif back to front on the adhesive side of the fabric, and draw around it with a fabric-marker pen. Cut out the motif.

ATTACHING THE APPLIQUÉ MOTIFS

Arrange the fabric motifs on the right side of the bag fabric. Peel off the adhesive backing; pin into place, then iron the motifs onto the fabric to fuse them, using a hot iron with a piece of fabric between the iron and motifs to prevent scorching. Once the motifs are firmly stuck in place, set the sewing machine to satin stitch (a tight zigzag in a small to medium stitch width), and sew around the edges of the motifs, covering all the raw edges.

MAKING UP THE BAG FLAP

Pin the front flap panel and matching lining panel with wrong sides together and machine-stitch along the bottom of this piece only (*see picture 1*). Press the seam open, then fold the fabric over so the right sides are facing, bring the top corners of the front panel and the lining panel together so that they marry up, and press again to create a crease along the longer lining panel, which will become the 2.5cm-wide border (*see picture 2*). Turn the fabric so that right sides are together again, and machine-stitch along the two sides of the flap, then trim away the excess seam allowance and snip diagonally across the corners. Turn the flap right side out, and steam-press flat (*see picture 3*). Topstitch along the top of the bag flap, securing the front and lining layers together.

MAKING UP THE BAG

Marry up the remaining pieces of outer fabric and their corresponding lining pieces – front panel, back panel and centre panel – and pin them all with wrong sides together.

Pin the front panel to the centre panel along the sides and bottom, making sure that the outer bag fabrics are facing each other, then machine-stitch all the layers of fabric together (*see picture 4*). Repeat the same process with the back panel (*see picture 5*). When the back and front panels are both attached to the centre panel, remove the pins that are holding the lining layer to the outer-fabric layer.

Trim the seam allowance to approximately 3–4mm, and snip the corners of the bag into a V shape. Turn the bag through to the right side, and steam-press.

FINISHING THE SIDE AND BOTTOM EDGES OF THE BAG

Topstitch the sides and bottom of the front panel to the gusset panel, then do the same for the back panel, sewing 5–6mm from the stitched edge, enough to miss the seam allowance on the inside of the bag. When you are topstitching the sides and bottom of the bag, make sure you stop short of the corners by 5–6mm, which will give you a neat folding edge (*see picture 6*).

5

6 7

JET-SETTING KIT

ATTACHING THE BAG STRAPS AND FLAP

Cut the webbing to the length you would like the shoulder strap to be, adding an extra 1cm seam allowance onto each end. To finish off the top edge of the bag, turn in both the lining and outer fabric by 1cm all around, and steam-press. Insert the raw edges of the bag flap 1cm between the outer fabric and the lining fabric of the back of the bag, with the outer fabric of the flap facing the outer fabric of the back panel, and pin in place. Insert the ends of the bag straps 1cm down between the outer fabric and the lining fabric of the gusset on each side of the bag, and pin them in place (*see picture 7*). Topstitch all around the top edge of the bag 2mm from the edge to secure the flap and straps in place, and create a neat edge along the front.

TRAVEL TIPS: If you are travelling by car, make sure that there is lots of fresh air, and praise your dog when he sits quietly in the car. (Use the travel blanket on page 104 to help your dog settle in the car.)

• If your dog suffers from motion sickness, don't give him any food just before or during the journey, but take plenty of water and don't forget to take regular rest stops so that he can stretch his legs and go to the toilet. (The water bowl on page 112 packs small and flat, making it ideal for journeys.)

• Always make your dog sit before you let him out of the car, so that he doesn't jump out into the road as soon as you open the door – use a treat to persuade him, if necessary.

• When you arrive at your destination, make sure that your dog goes to the toilet before he goes inside, to avoid any accidents, as he may be anxious or overexcited in new surroundings.

• In an unfamiliar environment, decide on a spot in which to put down his blanket straight away, so that he knows where his rest place is.

OVERNIGHT BAG

TRAVEL BLANKET

Essentially a comfort blanket for when a dog is away from home, this travel blanket is a great accessory for any dog owner. I always pack one when I travel with either of my dogs, and I also take one with me to meetings, so that my dog can settle down confidently no matter where he is. I have designed the blanket to be lightweight, so that it takes up as little space as possible and can be folded flat to fit into your luggage or rolled up in your handbag or pet carrier. I used 100 per cent cotton fabric and a soft, comfy fleece for the backing – my choice is always a printed fabric to contrast well with a plain, cushioned backing fabric, but you can use any fabric of your choice.

MATERIALS
- Pattern paper
- Tape measure
- Scissors for paper and fabric
- Patterned cotton fabric for the top panel
- Fleece fabric for the backing
- Pins
- Sewing machine and thread
- Centrefold bias binding in a matching colour

CUTTING OUT THE FABRIC

Decide how large you would like your blanket to be. Do this by cutting a large piece of pattern paper, sitting your dog in the middle and drawing a rectangle 15–20cm away from his body all the way around. Your dog should have enough space to lie down on his side. As a guide, my blanket sizes are as follows: small 60 x 50cm; medium 100 x 60cm; large 120 x 100cm. Cut a paper pattern to your chosen size, fold it in half and in half again, then draw a curve across the corner with the four cut edges. Cut out the curve so that when you open out the paper you will have a rectangle with four evenly curved corners. Use the pattern to cut out a top and bottom panel in patterned cotton fabric and fleece. Cut a 4 x 90cm strip of each fabric for the strap.

MAKING UP THE BLANKET

Place the top and bottom panels together with wrong sides facing, and pin them in place. Machine-stitch the two fabrics together, keeping as close to the edge as possible so that the stitching will not show outside the bias-binding edging (**see picture 1**).

Once the two panels have been sewn together, pin the centrefold bias binding all the way around the edge of the blanket, encasing the raw edges. Start in the centre of one side of the blanket, and ease the bias binding around the curved corners. Leave enough hem allowance to overlap the ends at the join before you cut the bias binding. Machine-stitch all the way around, sewing as close to the edge as possible, but making sure that you catch both sides of the bias binding within the line of stitching (**see picture 2**).

MAKING UP THE STRAP

Roll up your blanket and check that the tie will be the correct length. Trim it if necessary, and cut curves around the corners of the ends to make it easier to attach the bias binding. Pin the cotton and fleece strips together with wrong sides facing, and machine-stitch all the way around. Pin bias binding around the edge of the strap, easing it around the corners and machine-stitching it close to the edge, as above for the blanket.

ATTACHING THE STRAP TO THE BLANKET

Lay the blanket out on your work surface with the right side facing upwards. Measure about 11cm from the corner along one short edge, and mark this position with a pin. Fold the strap in half to find the centre point, and mark this with a pin. Pin the strap right side up onto the blanket at the marked points, making sure that it is perpendicular to the edge of the blanket (**see picture 3**). Machine-stitch across the strap, matching the stitch line attaching the bias binding underneath.

JET-SETTING KIT

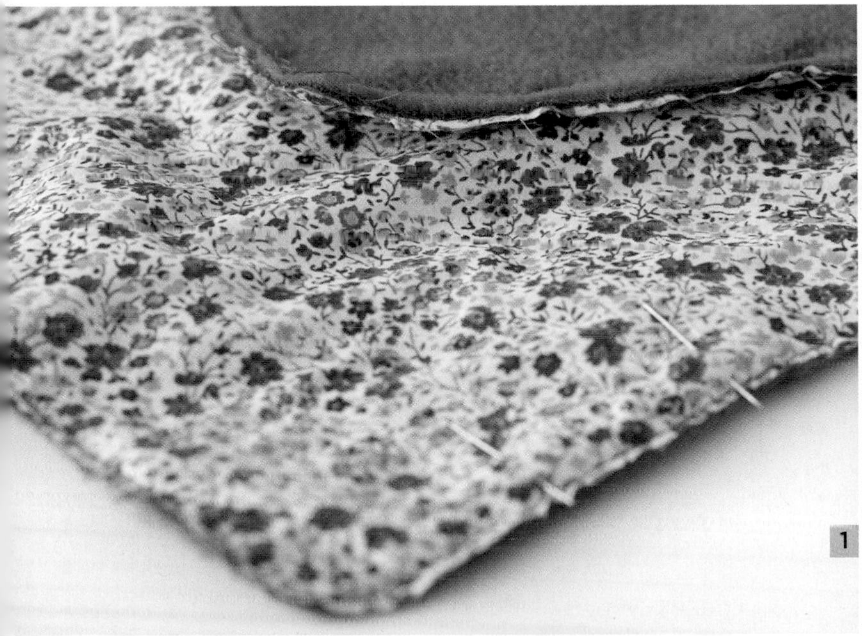

1

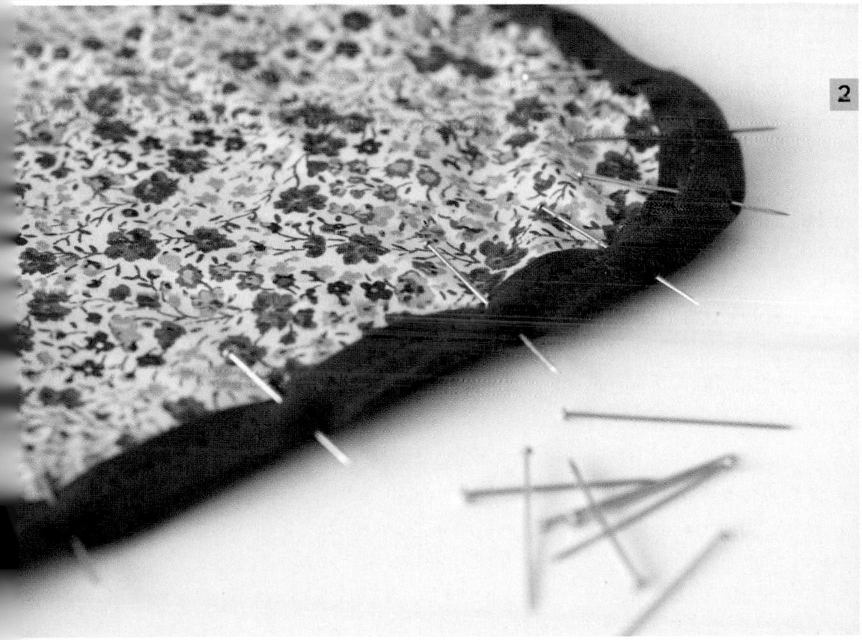

2

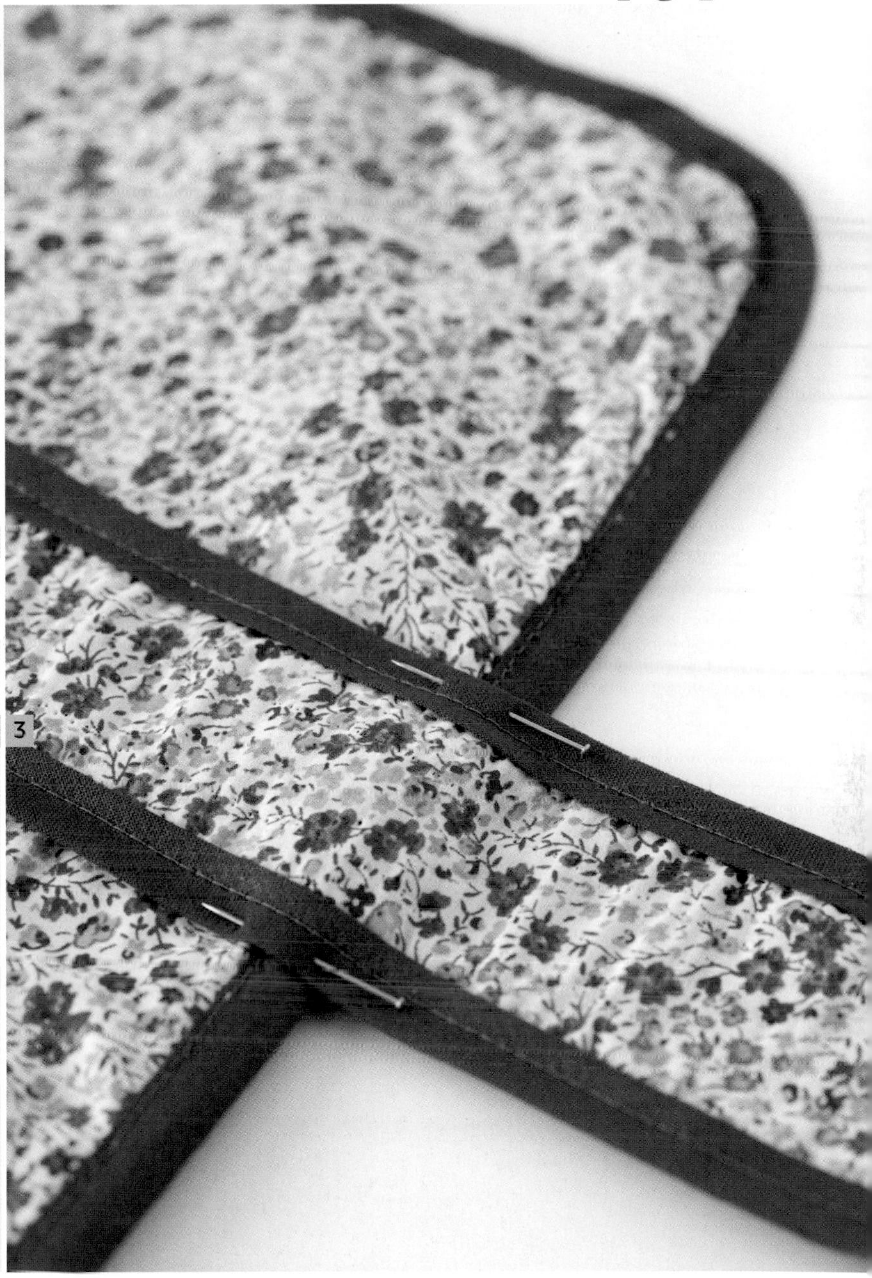

3

SAFARI JACKET

Your dog will know that it's holiday time when you get out his safari jacket. He will have figured out that something is going on once the suitcases are out, and he will be reassured to know that he is coming with you. As always, it is best to use a breathable natural-fibre fabric for this holiday jacket, such as cotton twill. It is practical and hardwearing, but will still pack up small enough for you to carry it in your bag all day, so you always have it to hand if the weather should turn cool or if you are still out in the evening when he might need some protection from a chilly breeze. Jack the terrier looks quite the intrepid explorer in his coat, ready for anything from sightseeing to hiking.

MATERIALS
- Pattern paper
- Tape measure
- Fabric-marker pen
- Adhesive tape
- Scissors for paper and fabric
- Cotton twill fabric in pale khaki for the main top coat
- Cotton twill in dark khaki for the belt and bias binding
- Patterned cotton lining fabric
- Hook-and-loop Velcro
- Pins
- Sewing machine and thread
- Iron and ironing board
- Belt buckle
- 2 buttons

TEMPLATES

C2 and B2 for the coat body and belly straps. Follow the sizing instructions for the tweed coat on pages 56–7.

A11, B11 and C11 for the pockets. Increase in size as desired. Add a 1cm seam allowance.
B1 and C1 for the collar and stand. Increase by 200 per cent, then increase or decrease accordingly to match the coat-body pattern. Add a 1cm seam allowance.

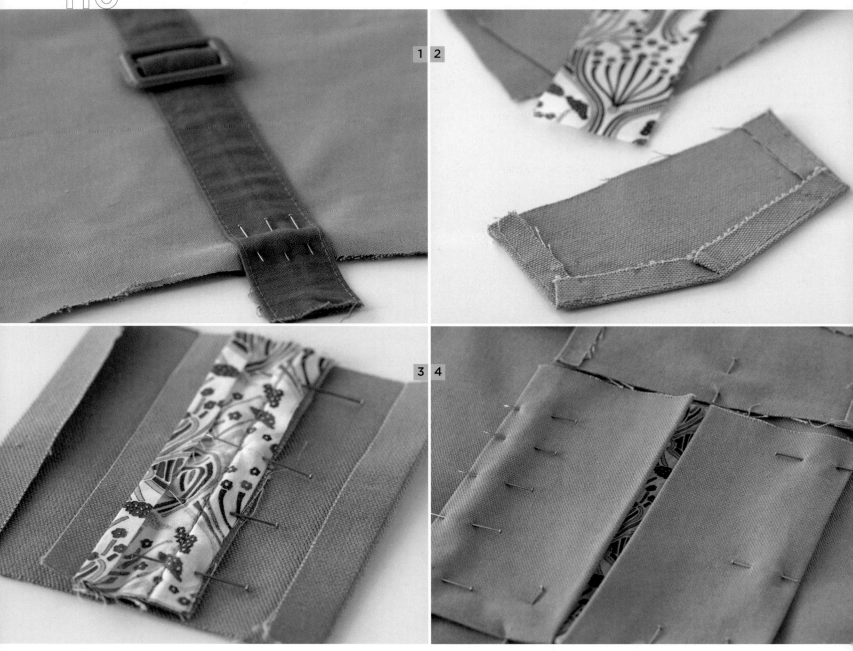

JET-SETTING KIT

111

CUTTING OUT THE COAT PIECES

Using the coat template on page 139 and referring to the instructions for the Country-Gent Tweed Coat on page 57, make a paper mock-up to fit your dog, and use this pattern to cut out the fabric as follows: 1 x main body with integral neck straps (in top-coat and lining fabrics); 2 x belly straps (in top-coat and lining fabrics).

Cut two strips of dark khaki cotton twill for the belt strap to the width of your buckle and the width of the coat, adding a 1cm seam allowance to both measurements.

Using the templates on page 142, cut out the left and right pocket panels and flap in pale khaki cotton twill and the middle pocket panel in lining fabric.

Using the templates on page 140, cut the collar and stand panels in the lining fabric and in the pale khaki.

ATTACHING THE VELCRO

Follow the instructions for the tweed coat on page 57 to sew Velcro onto the neck and belly straps.

PREPARING THE BELT STRAP

Pin the strips together with right sides facing, and machine-stitch, leaving a gap for bagging out. Turn through, press and topstitch 2–3mm in along both long edges. Push the belt loop through the strap to the centre, and stitch each end of the belt onto the sides of the top coat, positioning it where the belly-strap markers are (*see picture 1*).

PREPARING THE POCKETS

Pin and press a 1cm hem allowance along the sides and bottom of the pocket flaps, then topstitch along the pressed edges to secure the hems in place (*see picture 2*).

Pin and press a 1cm hem along the sides of the three pocket panels. With right sides together, pin the patterned middle section to the right and left panels. Machine-stitch, then press the seams (*see picture 3*). Lay the pocket right side up, and, from the middle, fold both side panels to the

centre to form a box pleat, almost covering the middle section; press. Pin and press a 1cm hem along the bottom edge of the pocket. Repeat for the other pocket.

ATTACHING THE POCKETS TO THE COAT PANEL

Position the pockets on the top coat, and pin. With right sides facing, line up the unhemmed edge of the pocket flap with the top edge of the pocket and machine-stitch to the coat (*see picture 4*). Topstitch 2–3mm in along the sides and bottom of the pockets to secure them to the coat. Fold the flaps down, press and topstitch; sew a button onto each.

MAKING UP THE COLLAR AND COAT

Refer to the instructions for the Velvet Smoking Jacket on pages 94–5 for making the collar, joining the top-coat and lining pieces, attaching the collar and edging the coat.

JET-SETTING KIT

PICNIC SET: BAG, BLANKET, BOWL & BALL

This picnic set is versatile and light, so it's easy to pack up in the matching bag to take with you on your travels, or use if you are having a barbecue or an afternoon in the park. Everything fits into the bag and still leaves plenty of space for your dog's favourite toys and food. The food bowl, which packs flat, is really useful for giving your dog water or dry food when you are on the move. The blanket can also be folded flat, or rolled up neatly. I chose a beautiful striped cotton twill in cheerful colours, along with contrasting red towelling, both of which are washable and hardwearing, so the blanket can double up as a towel if your dog fancies a paddle or an impromptu swim.

MATERIALS
- Pattern paper
- Tape measure
- Fabric-marker pen
- Scissors for paper and fabric
- Striped cotton twill fabric
- Contrasting red cotton fabric for the lining (or use the striped cotton twill)
- Iron and ironing board
- Pins
- Sewing machine and thread
- Contrasting red waterproof fabric for the bowl
- Contrasting red towelling fabric for the blanket and the ball
- Toy stuffing for the ball

TEMPLATES
A6, B6, C6 and D6 for the picnic bowl. Increase the templates by 400 per cent, then by another 115 per cent for a size small/medium. Thereafter, increase to suit. E7 for the picnic ball. Increase the template to suit the size of your dog. Add a 1cm seam allowance.

PICNIC BAG: CUTTING OUT THE PICNIC BAG PIECES

Cut out the following pieces of fabric, adding a 1cm seam allowance throughout: 2 x front and back panels in lining fabric, 38 x 26cm (mark out guide notches on your paper pattern to make it easier when marrying up the panels); 2 x front and back panels in outer fabric, 38 x 34cm (mark a fold line from left to right across the paper pattern, approximately 4cm down from the top, for the inner facing fold line); 2 x straps in outer fabric, 6 x 128cm; 1 x centre panel in lining fabric, 8 x 90cm (mark a fold line on your paper pattern approximately 26cm in from each end of this panel to help when marrying up); 1 x centre panel in outer fabric, 8 x 106cm (mark two fold lines on your paper pattern, the first 4cm in from the edge and another 30cm in from the first. Do this for both ends of the panel, to guide you when marrying up the centre panel to the front and back panels).

MAKING AND ATTACHING THE BAG STRAPS

Fold the two strips of fabric in half lengthways, and steam-press to form a central crease. Open the strips out again and fold both edges into the central crease, and steam-press. Fold the strips in half, folded edge to folded edge, and topstitch along the edge to hold them in place (see instructions for the sou'wester ties on pages 62–3). Pin one strap onto the right side of the front panel of the bag and the other onto the right side of the back panel, about 6cm in from each side, and machine-stitch (**see picture 1**).

MAKING UP THE BAG

With right sides together, pin the front of the bag to the centre panel, and machine-stitch along both sides and the bottom using a 1cm seam allowance. Pin and machine-stitch the back panel to the centre panel in the same way (**see picture 2**). Press the seams open. Repeat for the lining.

Turn the outer bag right side out and insert into the lining, with right sides together. Marry up the top raw edges of the outer bag and lining, and pin together. Machine-stitch along both long sides and one short side of the bag top using a 1cm seam allowance, leaving a gap of approximately 8cm on one short side (**see picture 3**).

Pull the outer bag through the gap in the seam, turning the lining right side out. Push the lining into the bag, and press a crease along the top seam of the bag, turning in the seam allowance at the gap as you do so, to give it a neat edge. Follow the placement lines on your pattern for the inner facing fold line.

Topstitch the outer bag to the lining approximately 3cm down from the top edge of the bag all the way around, locking both layers together (**see picture 4**). Steam-press the bag neatly.

PICNIC BOWL: CUTTING OUT THE PICNIC BOWL PIECES

Using the templates on page 140, cut out all the fabric pieces in waterproof lining fabric and outer cotton twill.

MAKING UP THE BOWL SHAPE

Fold the outer-fabric side panel in half with right sides together, and pin the ends together. Machine-stitch using a 1cm seam allowance. Repeat for the waterproof-lining side panel. Press the seams open (**see picture 5**).

With right sides together, pin and machine-stitch the bottom circular panel to the side panel on both the outer and lining fabrics (**see picture 6**). Turn both pieces right side out and topstitch the seam allowances to the side panels so that the seams lie flat when the lining and outer fabric are sewn together.

MAKING THE SIDE TOGGLE

Fold, press, and machine-stitch the strip of waterproof fabric in the same way as the bag straps, described above. Fold the strip in half, and stitch the ends together to form a loop.

ASSEMBLING THE BOWL

With wrong sides facing, place the lining into the outer-fabric bowl, and pin both layers together along the top edge. Pin the loop at the top of the side seam, aligning the raw ends with the top of the bowl. Machine-stitch all round, securing both layers and the loop (**see picture 7**).

Fold the waterproof bias strip in half around the raw edge of the bowl. Topstitch in place approximately 2mm from the edge of the bias strip, to encase the top rim (**see picture 8**).

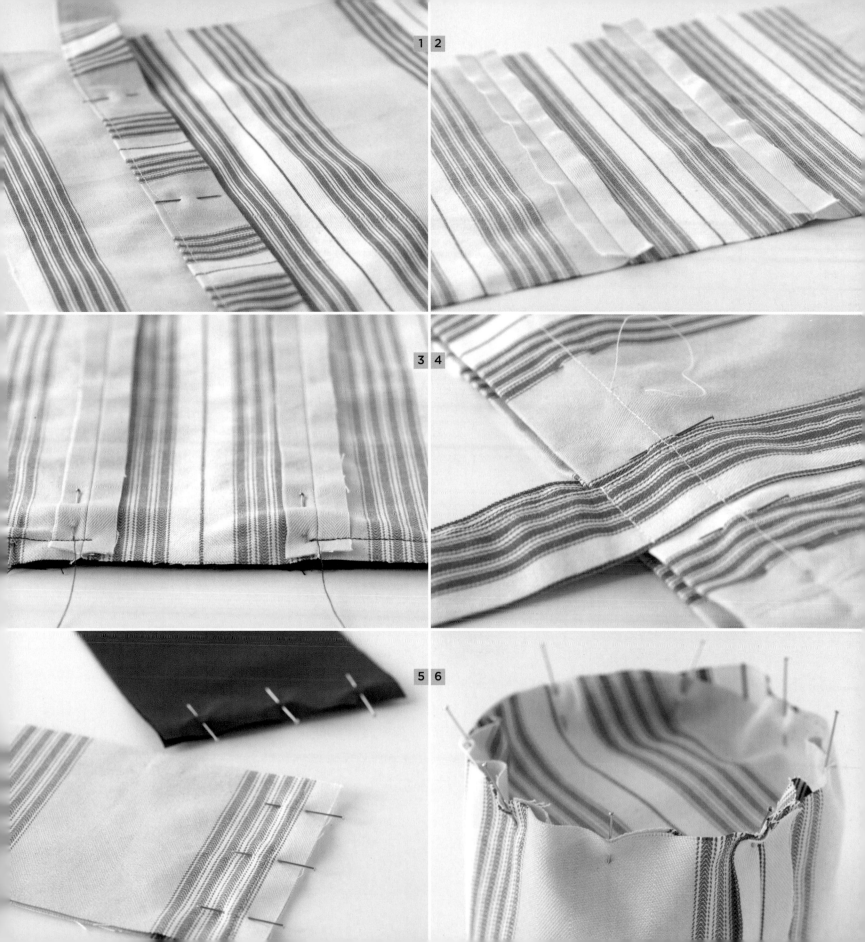

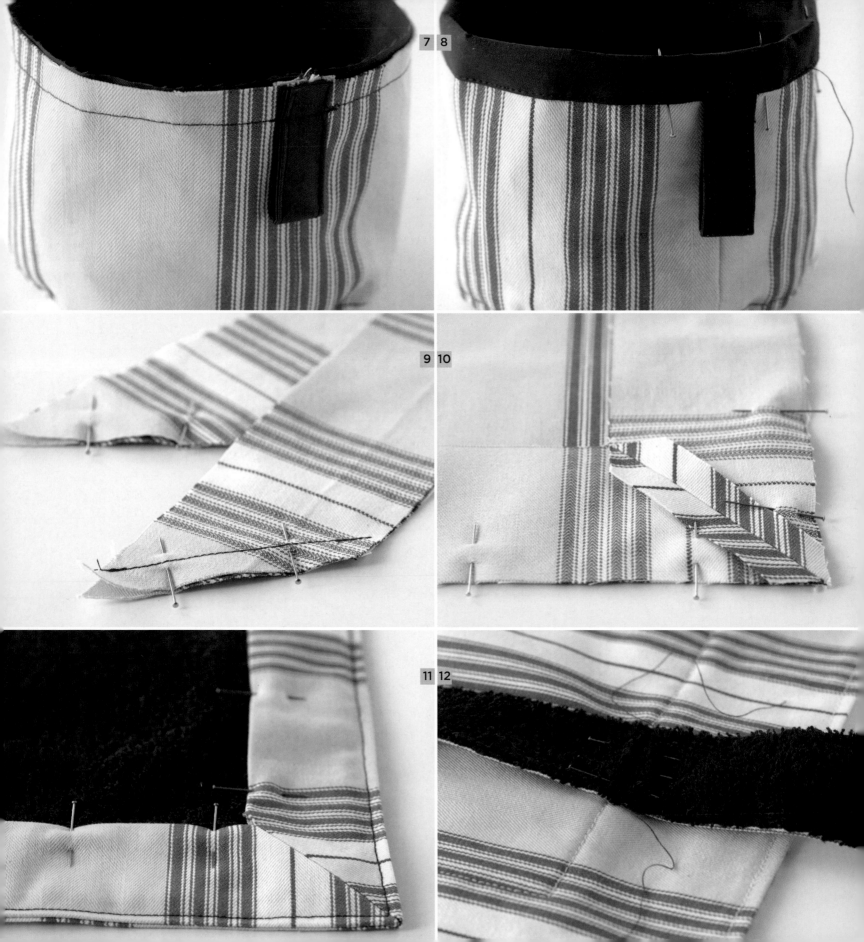

PICNIC BLANKET: CUTTING OUT THE BLANKET PIECES

Cut out 1 x top panel in towelling fabric, 42 x 32cm, adding a 1cm seam allowance. Cut out the following pieces of cotton twill fabric, making sure you cut straight on the grain of the fabric so that the stripes are straight. Add a 1cm seam allowance throughout: 1 x bottom panel 48 x 38cm; 2 x corner frame edgings for the side border pieces – top length 48cm, bottom length 42cm, width 3cm (when drawing out the 42cm bottom line, centre it directly 3cm below the 48cm top line, and join the ends of the top and bottom lines with a diagonal line to form a frame shape); 2 x corner frame edgings for the end border pieces – top length 38cm, bottom length 32cm, width 3cm (cut as described above). Put notch marks on your top/bottom panel against your border edgings, to make it easier when marrying up the panels later.

MAKING UP THE BORDER

With right sides facing, pin together a short and a long border piece at one end, and do the same for the other two border pieces. Take the short end of one set, and pin it to the long end of the other set; do the same for the other two border ends. You should now have what looks like a frame. Machine-stitch all the corners together using a 1cm seam allowance (**see picture 9**). Steam-press the seams open, and snip open the stitching from the inside corners of the frame by approximately 1cm – this will enable you to fold back the seam allowance along the edges later.

ATTACHING THE BORDER TO THE BOTTOM PANEL

Pin the border to the bottom panel with right sides facing. Machine-stitch around the outer edge using a 1cm seam allowance. Snip the corners diagonally to cut away the excess fabric, to give you neat, flat corners when you turn the border through (**see picture 10**). Turn the fabric right side out, and press to create a crisp edge. Topstitch the two layers approximately 5mm in from the edge.

ATTACHING THE CENTRE PANEL

Press under the 1cm seam allowance on the inner raw edge of the border. Insert the top towelling panel, tucking it neatly into the corners. Pin in place, and machine-stitch all the layers together approximately 5mm in from the inner folded edge of the border (**see picture 11**).

MAKING UP AND ATTACHING THE TIE

Pin the towelling and cotton twill strips with right sides together. Machine-stitch around the two long sides and one end, leaving the other end unstitched. Turn the strap right side out. Trim the corners of the unsewn end, and fold in the seam allowance, then topstitch all the way around the strap approximately 5mm in from the edge. Position the strap on the back of the blanket 10cm in from one corner, and topstitch securely (**see picture 12**).

MAKING UP THE PICNIC BALL

Using the template on page 140, cut out 3 pieces in each fabric. Pin a piece of each fabric with right sides facing, and machine-stitch down one side, using a 1cm seam allowance on the side and both ends. Join the other pieces in the same way until you come to the last seam. Then sew a line from each end, leaving a 5cm gap in the centre of the seam. Turn the ball shell right side out, and feed the stuffing through the gap in the seam. Fold back the seam allowance; pin then hand-sew the gap together (see Toy Bone on pages 28–9).

PICNIC SET: BAG, BLANKET, BOWL & BALL

BED & BATH

Dogs deserve the best comforts to
ensure that they get a good night's sleep.
My dog adores bathtime, and it's fun to watch
him splash about in the water, then wrap
him up in his towelling bathrobe to give
him a big cuddle. The pampering can continue,
as he stretches out on his luxurious bed or
curls up around his hot-water bottle.

BED & BATH

COMFY BED

This gorgeous circular bed will ensure that your dog can always rest comfortably and have a great night's sleep. It can be made in three sizes – small (63cm diameter), medium (90cm diameter) or large (108cm diameter). To choose the correct size for your dog, measure his approximate length when he is lying down on his side with his legs stretched out in front of him. The bed should be large enough for your dog to be able to stretch out on his side. I prefer to use a hollow-fibre cushion insert, as it keeps him cool in the summer and warm in the winter; it is also lightweight and easy to wash. Use a hardwearing fabric for the top and bottom panels, and a contrasting pattern for the border.

MATERIALS

- Tape measure
- Circular hollow-fibre cushion insert
- Scissors for fabric
- Cotton twill fabric for the top and bottom panels
- Contrast Liberty-print cotton fabric for the border
- Zip, half the circumference of your cushion
- Pins

- Iron and ironing board
- Sewing machine (with zipper foot) and thread
- Cotton string/cord for the piping, twice the circumference of your cushion plus 20–24cm extra
- Flat bias binding 40mm wide, length twice the circumference of your cushion plus 20–24cm extra

CUTTING OUT THE FABRIC

Measure your dog when he is lying down to work out how large a bed you need to make (see page 121), and buy a hollow-fibre cushion of the appropriate size. Cut two circles in cotton twill to the same diameter as the cushion insert for the top and bottom panels, adding a 1cm seam allowance all around. Measure the circumference and depth of your cushion insert – this will give you the total length and width of your border panel. Cut one piece of Liberty-print cotton to this width and half this length, adding a 1cm seam allowance all around. Cut another piece for the second border panel to the same length, but increase the width by another 2cm in addition to the 1cm seam allowance already added. Cut the wider panel in half to form two long strips (you will insert the zip into this section of the border).

INSERTING THE ZIP INTO THE BORDER

Fold down and steam-press a 1cm hem allowance on one side of your half-border panels where the zip is going to

go (**see picture 1**). Turn the two strips of fabric right side up, and pin one folded edge to each side of the zip, aligning the folds with the centre of the zip. Using the zipper foot on your sewing machine, sew all the way along both sides to secure the zip in place between the half-border panels. You will now have two border panels the same width, one with a zip and one without.

MAKING UP THE PIPING

Cut two lengths of string or cord to the circumference of the cushion insert plus an extra 10–12cm for seam allowances. Cut two lengths of bias binding to the same measurement. Place the string inside the bias binding, and pin it in place. Machine-stitch to secure, sewing as close to the string as possible, so that you have a good hem allowance on the bias binding (**see picture 2**).

MAKING UP THE BORDER

Join the two border panels together at one end only, to make one long piece of fabric which is the border section (**see picture 3**).

MAKING UP THE BED

With right sides together and the enclosed cord of the bias binding sandwiched between the two layers, start pinning the border panel onto the circular top panel (**see picture 4**). When you have worked all the way around the circle and the two ends of the border panel meet, machine-stitch the three layers of fabric (the top, piping and border) together, using a 1.5–2cm seam allowance.

Attach the bottom panel to the other edge of the border in the same way, pinning the second strip of piping between the two layers. Machine-stitch as before.

Finally, when the border panel has been joined to the top and bottom circular panels, trim off any excess border fabric where the two ends meet, fold the overlapping end under and hand-sew a vertical seam to finish.

HOT-WATER BOTTLE COVER

Keep your dog warm with a hottie overnight or on chilly winter days. You can put it on their bed or blanket, so they can curl around it when they are napping. Puppies and older dogs feel the cold a lot more than healthy adult dogs, and this is a simple way to keep them cosy. The cover is made from a soft wool fabric that is comfy for them to lie against and will ensure that the water bottle doesn't feel too hot. I have appliquéd the design with small, tight zigzag stitch, which is a lot easier and quicker than the satin-stitch appliqué method. I haven't used any Velcro on the opening of the hot-water bottle cover, but you can easily do that if you would prefer it to have a fastening.

MATERIALS
- Small hot-water bottle
- Tape measure
- Pattern paper
- Fabric-marker pen
- Scissors for paper, fabric and appliqué
- Adhesive tape
- Soft wool fabric for the cover
- Pins
- Sewing machine and thread
- Iron and ironing board
- Tracing paper
- Pencil
- Thin card for templates
- Fabric scraps for the appliqué motifs
- Contrast embroidery yarn
- Embroidery needle

TEMPLATES
A8, B8 and C8.
As a rough guide, enlarging the template in the region of 200 per cent will give you a pattern for a small hot-water bottle. Sizes of hot-water bottles do vary, however, so make sure you check that the paper pattern fits your hot-water bottle by taping the paper template together and checking the fit before you cut out the fabric.

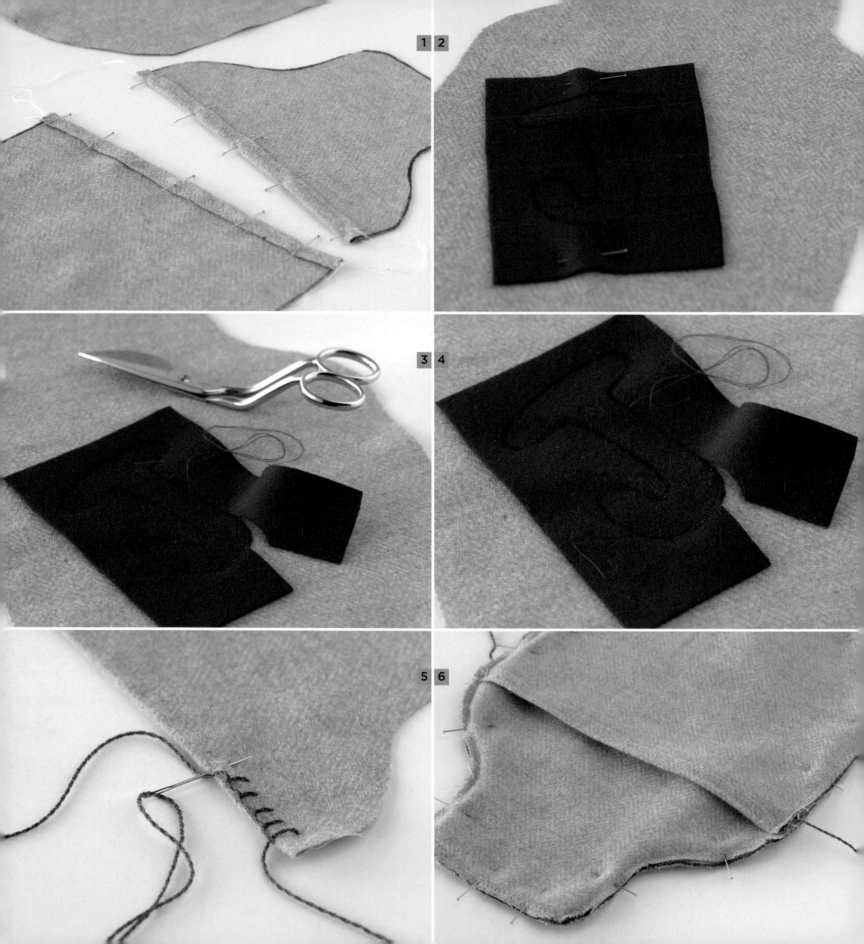

CUTTING OUT THE FABRIC

Enlarge the template on page 141 to the correct size
for your hot-water bottle (see page 124). Make a paper
mock-up, and check the fit against your hot-water bottle,
trimming the outline as necessary, but making sure you
leave a 1cm seam allowance all around. Use your paper
pattern to cut out the three fabric pieces that form the
hot-water bottle cover: 1 x front panel; 1 x top back panel,
1 x bottom back panel.

HEMMING THE BACK PANELS

Pin and machine-stitch 1cm hems along the straight
edges of the two back panels. Press the hems flat. These
form the gap where you will insert your hot-water bottle,
once the cover is complete (*see picture 1*).

CREATING AND SEWING ON THE APPLIQUÉ MOTIF

Choose the appliqué motifs you would like to use to
decorate the hottie, and enlarge them on a photocopier
(see page 138). I used two initials, and a bone, heart and
spot. Using tracing paper and a pencil, trace around the
shapes, transfer them onto thin card and cut out the card
templates using paper scissors. Trace the shapes onto
your chosen appliqué fabric. Making sure you leave at
least 2–3cm around the design you have drawn, cut out
a square of fabric, and pin it onto the right side of the
front panel of the hottie (*see picture 2*). Using small,
tight zigzag stitch, sew around the drawn outline of the
motif. Trim away the excess fabric using appliqué scissors
(*see pictures 3 and 4*). Repeat this process for all the
embellishments you want to have on the hottie.

BLANKET-STITCHING THE OPENING

Using a needle and 2 strands of contrasting embroidery
thread, work blanket-stitch edging along the bottom
hem of the upper back panel. Using the machine-stitched
line as your guide, bring the needle out to the front of
the fabric very close to the edge. Put the needle in
on the stitch line, one space to the side, and bring it
through to the front again over the top of the working
thread (*see picture 5*). Continue all the way along the

hem, spacing the stitches evenly. To finish, secure the
thread by making a tiny stitch on the edge.

MAKING UP THE HOT-WATER BOTTLE

Lay the front panel on your work surface, right side up.
First marry up the top back panel, with wrong side up, and
pin in place (this will be on top when the cover is right
side out). Next, pin the bottom back panel in place, and
machine-stitch all the way around the edge (*see picture 6*).

TOWELLING BATHROBE & MATCHING TOWEL

Even though he enjoys a bath, I don't wash my dog unless I really have to, so that he doesn't lose the natural oils in his coat, which protect him from the climate and when swimming in the lake or river. All of us dog owners know, however, that all dogs, whether they live in the town or the country, love rolling in disgusting, smelly things whenever they get the opportunity. When I have to bathe him, I use a natural, very gentle shampoo that doesn't strip the coat of its natural protection. After patting him dry with the matching towel, I use the towelling bathrobe to keep him snug and warm until he dries off completely. He loves snuggling into the hood and rubbing his ears dry with his paws.

MATERIALS
- Tape measure
- Fabric-marker pen
- Pattern paper
- Scissors for paper and fabric
- Adhesive tape
- Plain towelling fabric for the bathrobe and central panel of the towel
- Contrast cotton fabric for the trimming on the bathrobe (or ready-made bias binding) and for the towel border
- Pins
- Sewing machine and thread
- Iron and ironing board

TEMPLATES
A3, B3, C3, D3 and E3. Increase the templates by 400 per cent, then by a further 115 per cent to start. From thereon, increase all the pieces as required, so that the centre of the bathrobe's body piece measures the same length as your dog's back. Add a 1cm seam allowance. Follow the sizing instructions for the tweed coat on pages 56–7.

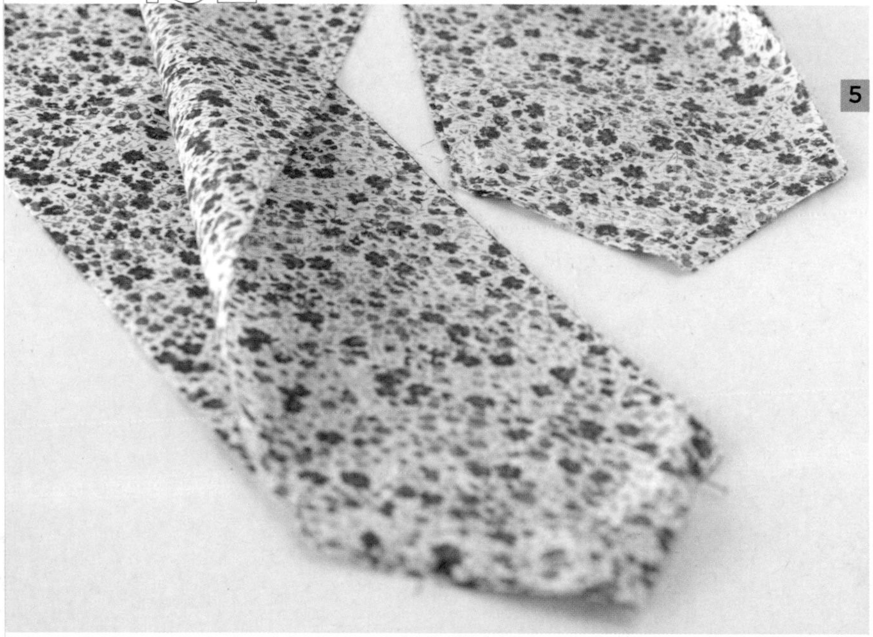
5

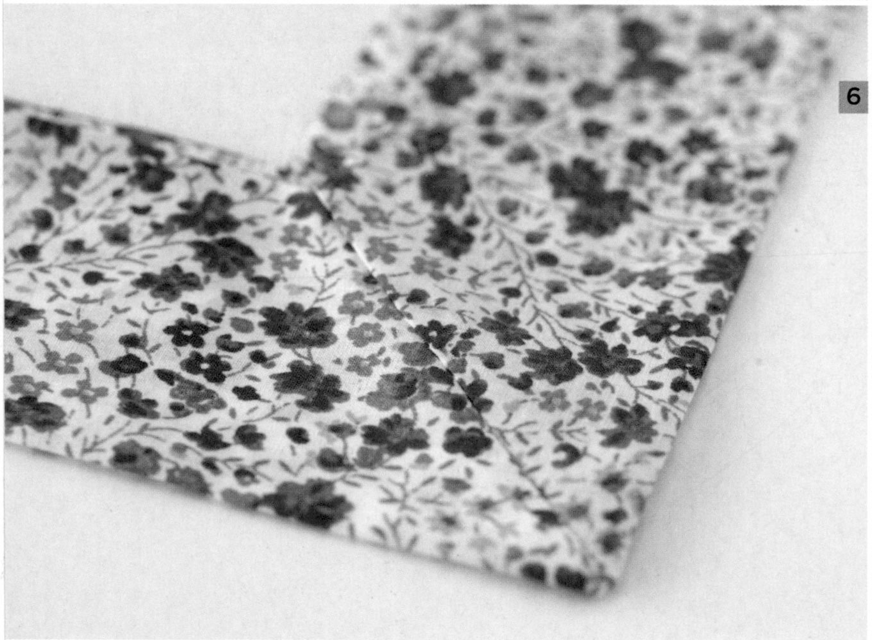
6

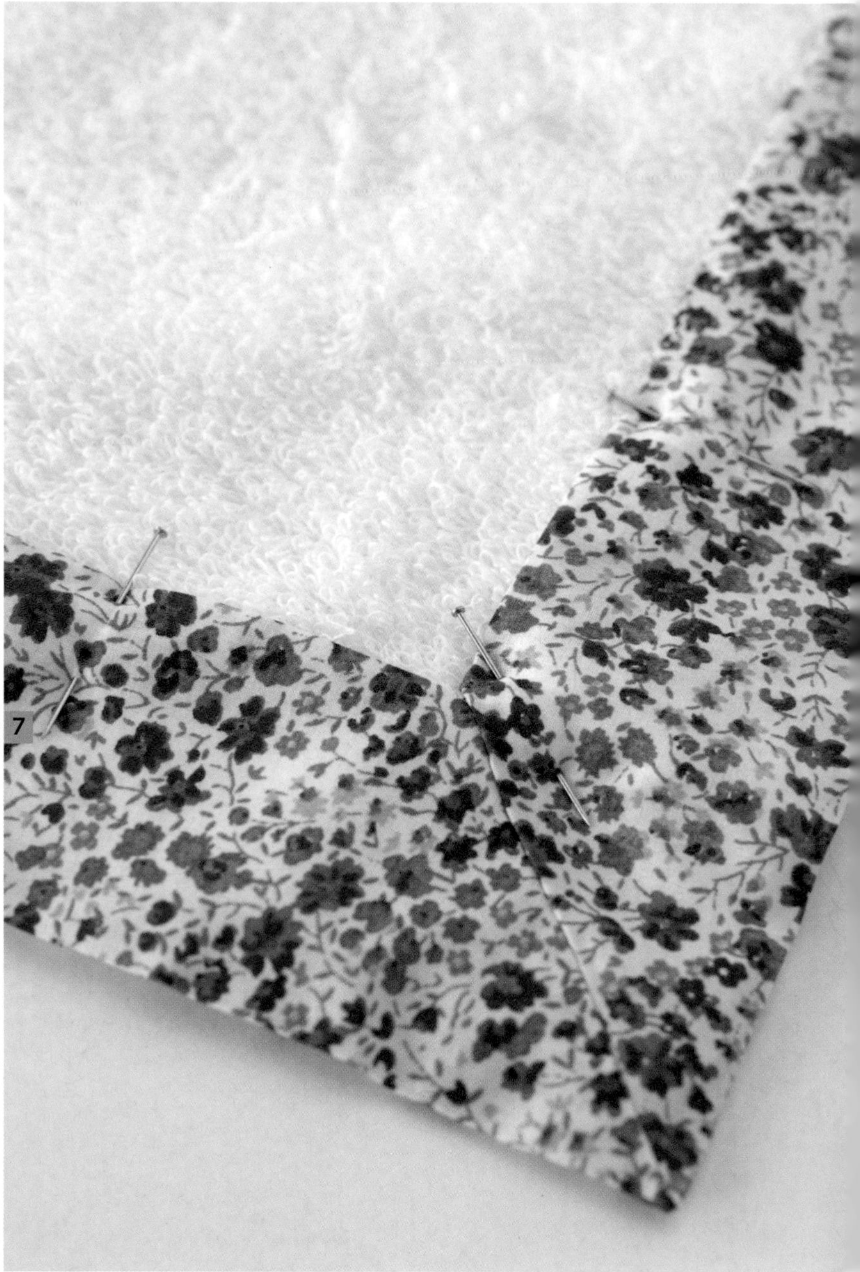
7

MATCHING BATH TOWEL: CUTTING OUT THE FABRIC

Cut out the fabric pieces for the central towelling panel and contrasting cotton border panels as follows, adding a 2cm seam allowance throughout: 1 x central panel in towelling fabric, 30 x 38cm; 2 x corner frame edgings for the side border pieces – top length 46cm, bottom length 38cm, width 4cm (when drawing out the 38cm bottom line, centre it directly 4cm below the 46cm top line, and join the ends of the top and bottom lines with a diagonal line to form a frame shape); 2 x corner frame edgings for the end border pieces – top length 38cm, bottom length 30cm, width 4cm (cut as described above). Put notch marks on your top/bottom panel against your border edgings, to make it easier when marrying up the panels later.

MAKING UP THE BORDER

Steam-press the four edging fabric pieces in half lengthways, creating a crease line down the centre. This crease will become the finished edge of the towel. Marry up the ends of one of the long edging pieces with one of the short pieces, and pin them with right sides together. Machine-stitch, leaving a 1cm seam allowance at either end, creating a V shape. Repeat the same process with the other two edging pieces (**see picture 5**). Join the two L-shaped pieces in the same way to form a frame. Trim the seam allowances, then turn the frame right side out. Your corners should come into shape easily because you steam-pressed the pieces down the centre line earlier. Where you left a 1cm gap at the end of each corner seam, fold back the 1cm seam allowance along both raw edges of the border edging. Start with one side at a time, and work your way around the frame, carefully steam-pressing the seam allowance back to create a neat finish. When you have pressed all the seam allowances back on the front and back of the frame, press the whole piece to even out any wrinkles (**see picture 6**).

SEWING THE FRAME ONTO THE CENTRE PANEL

Carefully separating the front from the back of the framework, ease the towelling centre panel into place until it sits comfortably within the frame. The edges of the centre panel should line up with the crease line on the edging. Pin through all the layers, working your way around the edges of the frame until the centre panel is securely attached to the frame (**see picture 7**). Topstitch a seam line all the way around the frame, sewing approximately 3mm in from the inner edge. Finally, steam-press the towel for a neat finish.

TOWELLING BATHROBE & MATCHING TOWEL

DOUBLE-LAYERED BLANKET

You can either use this cosy blanket to make your dog's bed even more inviting or throw it over your sofa to protect it from dog hair, keep it in the car so your dog is comfortable on journeys, or just spread it out on the floor by your bed or wherever your dog's favourite rest place is. The warm Sherpa fleece top layer is backed by cotton moleskin and trimmed with smart tweed to create a cushioned edge that makes the blanket feel extra snug. I recommend using good quality 100 per cent wool for the edging, as this wears best. The appliqué decoration gives the blanket a quirky touch, allowing you to personalize it with your dog's name or initials if you wish.

MATERIALS

- Tape measure
- Scissors for fabric and paper
- Sherpa fleece for the top panel
- Cotton moleskin or any other heavy-duty cotton for the backing
- Wool fabric for the edging
- Tracing paper
- Pencil
- Thin card for templates
- Fabric scraps for the appliqué (avoid jersey fabrics that stretch)
- Iron-on adhesive
- Iron, ironing board and ironing cloth
- Fabric-marker pen
- Pins
- Sewing machine and thread
- Needle and tacking thread

CUTTING OUT THE FABRIC

First cut out the fleece and moleskin fabrics for the top and bottom layers of the blanket – this blanket measures 60 x 100cm. Then cut out the 4cm-wide wool edging strips for all four sides of the rectangle – cut 2 x lengths of 100cm plus a 4cm seam allowance for each end (108 x 4cm) and 2 x lengths of 60cm plus a 4cm seam allowance for each end (68 x 4cm). If you want to increase the size of the blanket, cut the rectangles 100 x 120cm, and cut two longer edging strips 128 x 4cm.

CREATING THE APPLIQUÉ MOTIF

Choose the motifs you would like to use to decorate the blanket (see page 138). Using tracing paper and a pencil, trace around the motifs, then transfer them onto thin card. Cut out the shapes using paper scissors. Following the manufacturer's instructions, back your chosen appliqué fabric with iron-on adhesive. Place the card motif back to front on the adhesive side of the fabric, and draw around it with a fabric-marker pen. Cut out the motif.

ATTACHING THE APPLIQUÉ MOTIF

Arrange the fabric motifs on the right side of the fleece (*see picture 1*). Once you are happy with the layout, peel off the adhesive backing, and iron the motifs onto the blanket, using a hot iron with a thin piece of fabric between the iron and the motifs to prevent scorching. Once the motifs are firmly stuck in place, set the sewing machine to satin stitch (a tight zigzag in a small to medium stitch width), and sew around the edges of the motifs, covering all the raw edges.

JOINING THE TOP AND BOTTOM PANELS OF THE BLANKET

Lay out the top and bottom pieces of the blanket on your work surface with wrong sides together. Align the edges and smooth the fabrics with your hands, so that they are lying flat with no gaps or creases. Pin the two panels together along all four sides, then machine-stitch 1–2cm in from the edge all the way around.

ATTACHING THE EDGING TO THE BACK OF THE BLANKET

Measure and pin a hem of approximately 1cm along one side only of each of the edging strips. Lay the blanket with the bottom panel facing up, and place the four edging strips on top, with the right side of the strips facing the back of the blanket and the unhemmed edges aligning with the blanket's outside edges, and pin in place (*see picture 2*). Machine-stitch along each edge to attach the strips to the blanket panels. You should have what looks like a picture frame attached to the back of the blanket.

MITRING THE CORNERS

For each of the four corners of the blanket, hold the outer corners of the two edging strips that meet and fold each one diagonally back on itself, making sure that there are no gaps between the two parts of the join. Press with an iron and, using a fabric-marker pen or tailor's chalk, draw a clear line along the crease (*see picture 3*). Machine-stitch along this line to join the two pieces, then press the seam open and trim the excess fabric, leaving a hem of approximately 2cm (*see picture 4*). Repeat for each corner of the blanket.

ATTACHING THE EDGING TO THE FRONT OF THE BLANKET

Turn the blanket over so that the fleece is facing up, and flip the edging to the front of the blanket – the 'picture frame' is now on the right side of the blanket. Pin the edging to the blanket at regular intervals of about 5cm, then tack all the way around, keeping close to the inside edge (*see picture 5*). Using an edging or zipper foot if it helps, machine-stitch along the inside of the tacking stitches, sewing as close to the inside edge as possible so that the hem doesn't come apart (*see picture 6*).

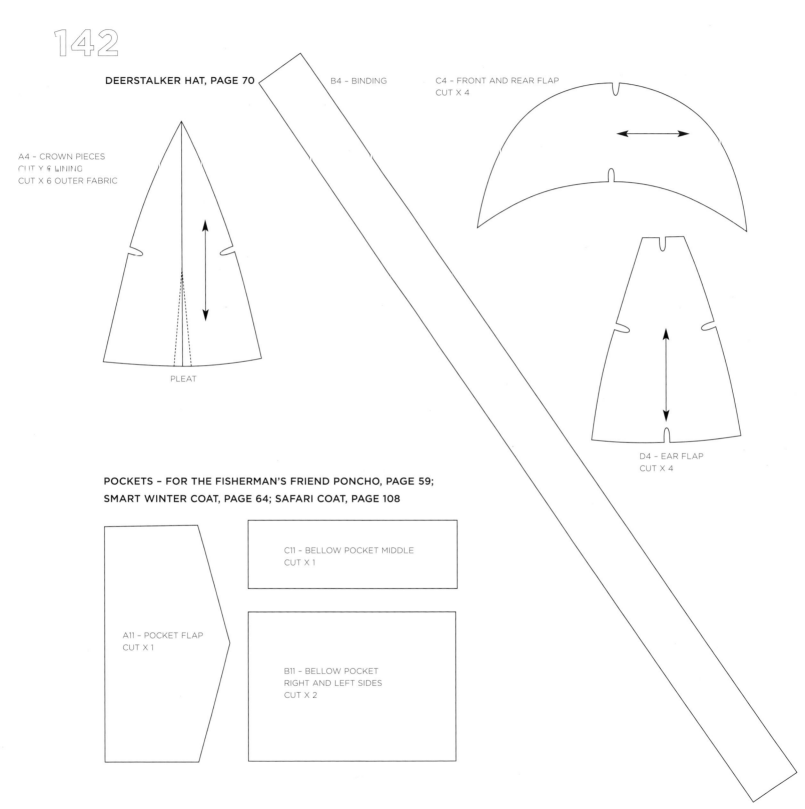

DEERSTALKER HAT, PAGE 70

A4 - CROWN PIECES
CUT X 6 LINING
CUT X 6 OUTER FABRIC

PLEAT

B4 - BINDING

C4 - FRONT AND REAR FLAP
CUT X 4

D4 - EAR FLAP
CUT X 4

**POCKETS - FOR THE FISHERMAN'S FRIEND PONCHO, PAGE 59;
SMART WINTER COAT, PAGE 64; SAFARI COAT, PAGE 108**

A11 - POCKET FLAP
CUT X 1

C11 - BELLOW POCKET MIDDLE
CUT X 1

B11 - BELLOW POCKET
RIGHT AND LEFT SIDES
CUT X 2

TEMPLATES

SOU'WESTER HAT, PAGE 59

BIRTHDAY T-SHIRT, PAGE 88

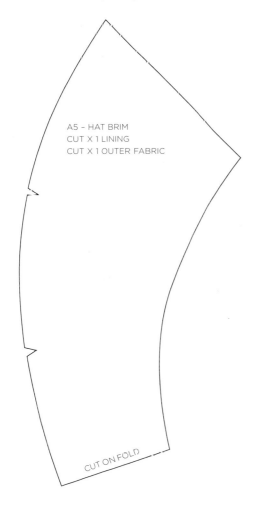

A5 – HAT BRIM
CUT X 1 LINING
CUT X 1 OUTER FABRIC

CUT ON FOLD

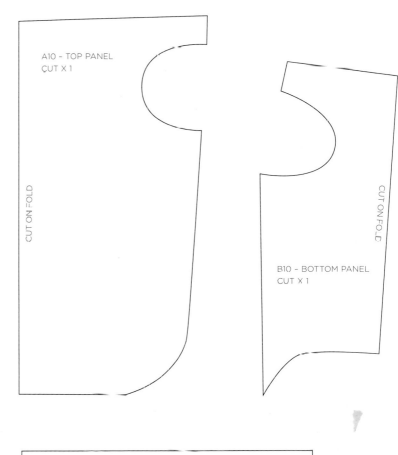

A10 – TOP PANEL
CUT X 1

CUT ON FOLD

CUT ON FOLD

B10 – BOTTOM PANEL
CUT X 1

C10 – NECK COLLAR PIECE
CUT X 1

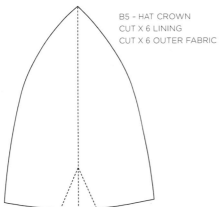

B5 – HAT CROWN
CUT X 6 LINING
CUT X 6 OUTER FABRIC

PLEAT

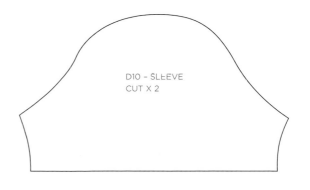

D10 – SLEEVE
CUT X 2

TEMPLATES